SIT WITH MONK XU

Spiritual Insights Training with a Modern Day Taoist Monk

MARIA PAU

DISCLAIMER

First Edition 2015

Copyright © 2015 by Maria Pau

National Library of Australia

ISBN: 978-099-243-791-6

Cataloguing-in-Publication entry:

Maria Pau, 1976

Xavier Attiig, 1975

Sit with Monk Xu: Spiritual Insights Training with a Modern Day Taoist Monk

1.   Taoism, Spirituality, Philosophy, World Religions, Monastic Living

Find Monk Xu at: www.MonkXu.com
Join Monk Xu on Facebook: www.facebook.com/MonkLife
Like Monk Xu's Facebook Page: www.facebook.com/XAQSHIN
Watch Monk Xu's YouTube Channel:
www.YouTube.com/TheMonkXu
Write to Monk Xu: X A Q SHIN Sanctuary
PO Box 260, Paradise Pt QLD 4216 Australia

Testimonials for Monk Xu

"When I first met Monk Xu to train I thought it would be like any other P/T session, I would push some weights around while chatting about my weekend and at the end I would be told what foods I should and shouldn't eat. After my first training session with Monk Xu I didn't speak as I walked away, my mind was still processing his words of truth and wisdom and my body was still in shock. This was how I would walk away from each training session with Monk Xu.

"Years may have passed since I last trained with Monk Xu but I still train my mind and body using the same techniques and lessons that Monk Xu passed onto me. Monk Xu taught me that training wasn't about pushing heavy weights or doing big curls, he taught me that we train to focus our mind and strengthen our body but most importantly, we train so when the moment comes we can help others. Training is a reward for the mind and body, not a punishment. I train as often as my mind and body allows, I make each session count, I push myself to the limit and then beyond—I am reborn after each training session. Monk Xu's training techniques have enabled me to train to a level where my mind and body can perform any task, from completing a marathon with no previous running experience to twice climbing in one of the most inhospitable and challenging environments on the planet— the Himalaya's.

"If you are fortunate enough to train with Monk Xu you will never be the same again, it is a rare life changing and truly humbling experience. I owe a debt of gratitude to Monk Xu that I will never be able to repay."

—Jaydon Mark Beatty

"Over the last few years our son has had major behaviour, anger and aggression problems, both at home and at school. Since our son has trained with Monk Xu in X A Q SHIN, his behaviour has greatly improved at school and made family time much more enjoyable. This is the result of a combination of guidance from Xu, fitness training and Qi Gong."

—Michael and Cheryl Mather

"Xu has given me many things, his time , his understanding, compassion and discipline. But of all the gifts I received; the most precious was 'Clarity in all things'. It had opened the door to change, the thing I feared the most. It's not just a training session; it's LIFE training."

—Ryan Cheney

"I have been fortunate enough in my lifetime, to have spent over a decade, having the experience of cultivating mind studies in the field of the 'KUNG FU' arena. During this time, I was also fortunate enough, to have trained with Monk Xu. Looking back at this amazing and some may say "unusual" time that I did train with Monk Xu, I can say first hand, that I witnessed an incredible metamorphosis within Xu.

"The nature of our training, indeed came from a man who was able to channel Dharma. From the many, many people that came through the hands of both mine, and Xu's teacher, in my opinion, not even a few were able to comprehend it... embrace it... and truly be it.

"For after all, the particular teacher was a hardened man, with a heart that was not particularly softened with love. A very good one nonetheless, but missing what is essential for the recipe of enlightenment... love, sincerity and compassion on all levels.

"So come the hundredth monkey, or nowadays the one in ten thousandth monkey... come monk... come Monk Xu. From my experience, I could never slot back, to being just another brick in the wall. I would never care too, but for the times I feel like I need to be reminded about what it is that I am... I turn to Xu. We are all love, we are all love from the Source, but not separate from the Source.

"We are the Source, and for those who struggle with everyday hazards of being infinite awareness in this sometimes cumbersome human body, Monk Xu is the one to alleviate ones suffering... to help put into perspective... and, to put oneself back in touch with this unconditional love. I highly recommend Monk Xu on many levels. For Martial Arts training, Qi Gong, Mind Studies, and just to feel the very moment itself. I call myself a very lucky person indeed, to call Monk Xu my soul brother."

—**Fiona J Croft**

Testimonials for Maria Pau

"Maria's method of coaching is beyond compare. She has helped me to realise my dreams and ambitions, and pinpoint exactly how I can turn them into reality. I was very unsure with what direction I wanted my life to lead, but with Maria's guidance, I have a clearer understanding of where I want to be.

"Maria is extremely passionate, committed and above all dedicated in ensuring I reach my full potential. Her enthusiasm and optimism is felt at every single coaching session I have with her. Maria, most importantly, puts my wants and desires into action.

"I feel that I am gaining invaluable knowledge from Maria about the specific aspects of my life I consider need improving. Maria gives me confidence and makes me feel completely comfortable when interacting with her. She strives for excellence, and I know already that she will keep motivating me to carry out my goals."

—Evelyn Vila

"Having Maria for a life coach has made a difference in my life. With Maria's help, I have been able to identify what it is I really want in life; set inspiring goals and begin to see ways to achieve them. Maria has helped me fall in love with the process of realising my dreams and so I am confident that by the end of my coaching program with Maria I will have achieved my goals no matter how ambitious they appear to be.

"Maria has played an important role in helping me feel a sense of balance in my life. The journey with Maria thus far has been amazing; I always look forward to my coaching sessions with Maria as I believe that coaching has allowed me to experience a more fulfilled and happier life. Maria is the best coach anyone could wish for—she is passionate, affirmative and a superb role model."

—Lynette Phuoung

"What an amazing lady. Interesting, smart and insightful. I like what she is trying to do. With her passion, I am sure we will hear much from her."

—Vicki McGuire

"Because of Maria's coaching, I realised that I have so much more of myself to develop and many times I will lose self-control and maybe even fall back into my vice. But because of our coaching sessions, I can easily recognise how my habits form and put a stop to it before it is too late. She is very supportive and it was humbling to have her help me heal a destructive life."

—John Ng

"Crossing paths with my coach Maria Pau was one of those encounters that changed my life. In the beginning, I had never heard of a life coach and I was in the middle of some very confusing times in my career. I was looking for a way to build a small foundation housing homeless workers in the Manila area and I was losing confidence that I could continue my project on the small donations I was able to gather. When Maria approached me for coaching, my understanding was that it would be a way to just get feedback and get to talk to someone about my challenges. How wrong I was! Having to be accountable for my weekly accomplishments and a confidant to help me balance out my decisions was exactly what I needed to cause a revolution in my life.

"I transformed a forty-bed dormitory from a charity to a social enterprise with a lower cost of $1.00 a night and a pioneering a work-for-stay method for those who could not pay. In the last three years it has grown into 1500 beds and has helped almost 95,000 people. My desire for higher education that I had put in the backseat for several years was revived and I started to scout for scholarships for students from developing countries. My work in the homeless shelters impressed the Architecture department in the Massachusetts Institute of Technology to give me fully paid one year tuition and living expenses.

"I am now entering Harvard University with a similar support package.

"In between, I was honoured by having my story covered by reader's digest and CNN and awarded as one of the youngest ever to receive the Ten Outstanding Young People of the World.

"By focusing my energies on priorities and a structure to see what was really important to focus on slowly helped me to focus my time and resources on the opportunities that were in front of me. What was important was having an energetic and positive coach to keep me on track even after every disappointment and showing me that it was all part of the process of success. Having Maria as a Coach and the breakthrough of Life Coaching is an investment that gives us the greatest return by unlocking our life's potential."

—Illac Diaz

"I was so nervous before ringing Maria. I have a learning condition that has really stopped me in my tracks and stunted my confidence. As I started working with Maria, we did so many great exercises that enabled me to learn better and have fun with it all. Now I book so many jobs and am so much more confident. Thanks to Maria's understanding & patience, my life is completely turned around. It was the best money I ever invested!"

—Rachael Hobbs

Introduction

Life, as we all know it, means that you were triumphant over a billion other cells that did not make it to form you. Uniquely YOU. You are already a miracle!

Then, the other life as we know it began. Dreams we've imagined since we were young, difficulties and struggles while trying to keep a roof over our heads. Many of us are still just trying to survive, to take care of our financial responsibilities and care for our dependents. Others are trying to do "right" in the eyes of their God, while some adore relaxation and laziness, a sort of social anarchy, where life seems quite pointless.

When we look around, taking in life for all that it is, we see addiction, struggle, death, ugliness, hatred, and many other things coined as "negative," and although we do see love, beauty, togetherness, harmony, and joy as well, it sometimes feels as if the "positive" is shadowed in the overwhelming nature of the evilness and cruelty of this world. So throughout life, I have been burdened with aching questions. These questions continued to overwhelm me in the face of the horrors and terrors I've witnessed.

We've seen and experienced many horrors, and sometimes even felt that life is pointless. You know those times when you think: We are all going to get old, get sick, and die; so, why try and follow our dreams? Why improve ourselves if the end result of all our improvement involves rotting away in a grave or burnt to ashes and cast off over the ocean. What is it about this life that makes it worth so much and what is this thing called our soul? Whether you believe in a God of your choosing, Nature, the Universe, or nothing at all. Finding balance, peace, and harmony always seems to be a constant struggle within this fast-paced, stress-driven, money hungry society we live in.

This book comes forth to simply present you clarity and a tool to better understand this mind that watches this world that we live in. Recorded from the words of my learnings, sitting at the foot of venerable Monk Xu. Founder and director of XAQ Shin Sanctuary in the Gold Coast, Australia. I can attest that he practices what he has learned from from modern day mystics such as Jiddhu & U. G. Krishnamurti, Chuang Tzu, Huang Po, Rumi, Takuan, Hafiz, Alan Watts, Bashar, Osho and Tabash.

He is well-read and cultured from his many astral encounters with this world and others. Taoism, Sufism, Kabbalah, balance, meditation, cultivation of a compassionate heart and harnessing the collective good are all explored to better understand the nature of the mind, body, and soul. This book will teach you that it is pivotal to still the mind and experience Who You Truly Are. From both Monk Xu and myself, we share our Love in the presentation of this book, and from both of our hearts, we hope you enjoy reading it just as much as we enjoyed writing it. This book is simple yet profound, each short chapter bringing you closer and closer to the Divine within.

—Monk Xu and Maria Pau

TABLE OF CONTENTS

Chapter 1

Windows to the World

Many people are alive but don't touch the miracle of being alive.

—Thích Nhat Hanh

Mind is used to see the totality of "All That Is"

What are those two dangling things that you stand upon, that bend upwards and downwards and can roll a few degrees to the right and left? Each has five pointing extensions that we call toes. Although this resembles one of those Taoist wordplays that students consider nonsense at first until the miracle of experience uncovers the truth, the answer is simple: *your* feet! Think of your feet. Bend your toes and take a deep breath. They feel nice, don't they? Little muscles are spread throughout the inside and along the ventral top; strong calcium-packed bones run from the calcaneus to a centimetre or two from the tip of your distal phalanges. Imagine walking without your feet, whereas your little nubs struggle and your legs tremor holding the entire weight of your body with each step. Thousands of people, perhaps more, base their walking on this experience, and I would guess most prefer the balance and comfort that prosthetic feet elicit.

For those with feet, jump up and down and feel your heart increase, tiny sweat droplets building underneath the surface of your skin. Go for a run and experience the wind brushing past your upper cheekbones. Your ankles bend and with force push off on the starting blocks of the 100-metre dash, transforming you from potential to kinetic.

Your feet are two little miracles, as normal as they seem to you and everyone else, and in the bigger picture of our lives flaunting with a constant flow of necessary tasks, our foot receive little attention, much less thanks for the role they play. Certainly thanking our own feet is an absurd idea, and let's not even begin with the importance of our hands, our tongue, eyes, nose, fingernails, and our more sensually pleasurable organs. Often we don't express continual gratitude for the components of our bodies, and in part it is because they are a section of what makes us physically whole. Our bodies exist as we exist, our hands move half the time without even thinking of it. Fortunately, we don't have to focus on our hearts beating to stay alive.

But even then, we don't refer to our body parts as a part of us. Instead, we express ownership of our hands, feet, eyes, intestines, and so on.

It's *my* feet.

My heart.

My ingrown fingernails that hurt like hell.

Hence, this ownership over our body implies an owner. You. Me. So, the point of arrival remains: who is this *you* and who is this *me* when the parts of our bodies are not considered to be a part of our being? In both Latin and Greek, *ego* is the word for *I*; in English, we designate *I* to mean the *self*. In respect of clichés and the owner of your guts, bodily extensions, and other organs, we now have to ask: who am *I*? What is *I*?

I am not my hands; I have hands.

Take a moment and try to imagine what part of your body would be your *I*, or as also called, your *ego*. If you are like most of us, I'm going to imagine that your *ego* would be right between the eyes and a little behind the forehead, the very same place where your thoughts manifest and display messages scrolling across what seems to be a typical scrolling marquee. It's not quite the brain, it owns the brain as well, and it is called the *mind*. Our environment and designates our inner activities and express this information in the form of thoughts—our mind is our window to the world.

But here is the problem: how clean is your window, or more specifically, how well can you see both *out* of your window as well as *in*? What is the state of your *mind*? The state and cleanliness of the mind is just as relevant today as it will ever be. There aren't many who wish to live in agonising fear, distress, unhappiness, jealousy, gluttony, dissatisfaction, loneliness, and thinking everything else in the world that basically *sucks*.

Beds are often warm and comfortable, soothing the heart and letting the conscious and subconscious revel, but the serenity of sleep is much too short in the world today. Interrupted by a screeching alarm clock, the harrowing *Beep! Beep! Beep!* of hell, and immediately the day ignites with a set of tasks that must get done. 15 minutes to shower in sleep deprived grogginess, soap splattered across the body, and 15 minutes to eat but no time to chew, breakfast forced down the throat in chunks so that the stomach growls in its annoyance, clothed, the keys in hand, and off to work for the day. At work, the mind is occupied by a range of tasks as well as finances, relationships, dreams of the future and memories of the past, desires, wants, needs, hunger and thirst, stress about the lack of time and the millions of things to do in our days, stress about our futures, whether we are living up to the goals that we set for ourselves, reflections on the political and economic nature of the world, the constant slamming of death, destruction, famine, poverty from the media, and the comedy and light-heartedness we can find on television and in our social interactions.

Basically, the striking colours of a sunset are simply electromagnetic radiation in the form of wavelengths sent out from the sun and hitting the limited colour sensitivities of our eyes. All across the globe, taking a moment from our busy and action-packed days to notice the robust reds shooting up over the mountains or spreading across the waves of the sea, the oranges reflected across scattered clouds, and the deep yellows colouring the rooftops and the sides of buildings, is one of the most beautiful experiences of life that serves to stop the world in its beauty, and no matter what individual people from France or Japan have going on, a beautiful sunset, no matter how many times it is seen, is a short moment of peace. Suddenly, the mind quiets down. You are no longer allowing your marquee to scroll at a hundred miles an hour. For a moment, life feels absolutely okay the way it is. You are perfect the way you are. And then the sun goes down and the mind starts again; the peace doesn't last, but for that short pause where you stopped to notice the beauty of a sunset, your mind was clear, calm, and quiet.

The mind is all there is, it is the window of how you experience the world, rationalise your life and plan your futures; the mind is where you remember your past; it was where we can describe the taste of a carrot or the pleasure of sex. In essence, the mind is in which you experience, to view the contents of the world that you exist in.

Your mind is certainly not your eyes; your mind is the awareness behind your eyes, watching. Your mind is not your ears or your nose; it is that awareness that captures the scents and sounds, allowing you to view the contents of the world. You are not your brain either, as the brain, a whole bunch of neural attachments, is simply the producer of thoughts.

If the mind is "dirty," packed with brain-constructed thoughts running like mad, as if each thought was a piece of confetti thrown upwards towards a spinning fan and scattered in every which way, then how well can we consider its ability to experience our environment? As much as many of us like to consider ourselves to be multi-taskers, the mind can only handle one thing at a time.

The Mind and the now dictate reality

It is exactly why the years seem to pass on by and dreams remain unfulfilled; why the journey from point A to B is forgotten, unnoticed. At times, many of us are caught so deep in all of the sensory attraction around us along with the constant thinking that we forget that we exist, that we are *here* right now at this very moment in space and time.

You only exist when you think of it.

Thought only exists when one thinks of it.

The mind is all there is.
The All Seer.
The All Seeing.
The All Seen.

When the mind, or awareness, is all there is, the same can be said for that moment right *now*. Thus, the *Now* is all there is. The ambient sounds around you at this very moment is the only reality that exists, the car horns, sounds of rubber racing against the street, the wind blowing along my window and through the trees surrounding my home, the smell of coffee on the pot, the computer in front of me, the task of writing this book.

These are all elements of my *Now*, my reality. Those arguments that I had in the past, where I remember crumbling in the moment and realised the perfect comeback ten minutes after the occurrence no longer exists except in my thoughts and memories.

The rent due at the end of the month, causing stress of an empty bank account, is an assumption and a future projection. Fearing an eviction of the future has nothing to do with the current reality, the *Now* that allows you to focus and think creatively to ensure a home over your head. The mind and the *Now* dictate reality, and the mind being your ego, your *I*, dictates who you are. And with one more essential connection to make—your brain, the producer of thoughts, makes it so that even your thoughts about the *Now*, your current reality, is not who you are.

When the brain's activity ceases to dictate, the mind watches and there is greater awareness of the universe.

There's more space, a cleaner window, an unlimited wonderment of mind.

This is the *I* we've been exploring throughout this chapter thus far. By being *who* you are, by being the awareness in the present moment, allowing the world as it is to showcase itself to you and you resolving in watching it in its entirety, without judgement or assumption. Peace will reign over you, and love and compassion will surely follow.

The mind as it is, the present moment and your soft awareness, brings you right into that feeling where you watch the sunset in tranquillity, where you see the lines on the road when a big block V-8 vibrates through your spine, giving you the sensation your brain perceives. You see a marquee of thoughts and none that keep you up at night in fear, stress, or worry. You feel it when the fan stops moving. You may relate it as every thought being confetti and when the fan stops, the confetti ceases to fly about and land gently on the ground. Each vibrant colour landing gently and you offer no judgement on whether the colour is beautiful or ugly.

Your dreams, your goals, your existence of the non-self and the no ego, with feet and hands and a beating heart that you express infinite gratitude for, with the horrors and celebrations of life exactly the way they should be to delineate your experience, this all comes down to the quiet mind, one that is fearless.

Throughout the duration of this book, as we explore subjects on spirituality, Taoism, the duality of the universe, and much more as presented by the venerable Monk Xu. It is our wish that it will be understood and put to practice, to enhance your life, through realisation of your non-self, cultivating the brilliant essence of the mind where stillness gets solidified by daily practice and by the embodiment and appreciation of all that is *Now*.

In other words, to understand a Monk and how you can reach the highest level of strength and compassionate cultivation, you need to understand the basic fundamental of who a Monk is:

A Monk is one who watches.

Another is to understand the will, strength, tolerance and overall courage a Monk cultivates within. A monk is a virtuous spirit of mastery who in all sincerity watches and falls not, into the hooks of illusion.

Let's say you have reached your peace. Now to be a leading example of that peace is another story. In all sincerity—Monk Xu always reminds me on how dedication comes into play especially when the hooks of others are consistently bombarding you and your surroundings.

Take a deep breath and simply listen. Observe, be present—never fall into the trap with opinions. Monk Xu gives me the greatest move when it comes to conflict. Simply walk away. Simplicity is the key to being effortless—especially when it comes to watching—watching all that there is.

Chapter 2

Diseases of the Mind

In today's rush we all think too much—seek too much—want too much—and forget about the joy of just being.

—Eckhart Tolle

The need for significance.

Being in the *Now* and fully aware, watching without judgement as the world remains exactly as it should be, doesn't necessarily eliminate the fear and darkness that are so profound in life. With a deep breath inwards, watching your lungs expand and fill with the oxygen of life-giving air, and through slowly releasing that air as it brushes against your lips, you may notice that the birds outside sing and a vanilla sky lazily rolls above your head, the *Now* and you simply existing can be peaceful and pleasant, focused and compassionately sincere.

As I mentioned in the last chapter, your moment and place in the *Now* is all there is, and that your mind is everything. However, while looking out the windows at the singing birds and shimmering sun, everybody singing songs like a feel-good Disney extravaganza, there are gunmen in western Ethiopia who ambushed a bus and killed nine civilians; men, women, and children bobbing up and down in the cold waters off South Korea after a ferry boat packed with Easter vacationers capsized; war brewing between Ukraine and Russia; the bloodiest war of our time continues to unravel in Syria, and that's just the first four news articles when I browse my online newspapers.

Sure, we can say that the newspapers aren't balanced in the way that Nature is balanced, and I would love to have every story on death, famine, and destruction accompanied by a story of peace, love, and togetherness, but media-sponsored fear helps us purchase extra locks for our doors, shut us away in our homes, and buy other things we don't need to make us feel better. Turn on the news on your television, and for 30 minutes you are bombarded with bullying, executions, human rights infractions, and *Fear! Fear! Fear!* Then, with all of the fear sent right into the awareness, a commercial break appears and it's *Buy to make your life better!*

You got pimples? Good luck finding love and happiness until you buy this facial cream.

See these people wrestling around and having fun with well-kept hairdos? You can be just as happy and full of love and life with the right clothes.

Freedom and independence on the open road only occurs when you're behind the wheel of the latest edition of this car. Don't you see yourself sitting in the drivers' seat with a well-endowed gal rocking a short skirt in the passengers' seat?

Even though the balance between *Fear* and *Love* on television is proportionate to an elephant and a pig on a weighing scale, doesn't mean that the so-called "horrors" of this planet do not exist. You would be quite naïve to sit there and believe that the entire world is as happy as you are when lying on green grass watching the clouds float by.

As your mind focuses on your surroundings, whether you are part of a "bad" experience or witnessing it second-hand, the moment that you start judging these occurrences as *bad* or *evil* takes you away from a peaceful and calm mind that simply watches. It is here that the assumptions you have, the virtues you hold, and the ideas of the world that you have been given or created take over and cloud the window in which you view and experience. This is where the world is created through thought, assumption, and imagination.

For example, when holding your hand over a burning candle, you have this whole slew of vocabulary and ideas about burning flesh and scorching skin to tell you that this activity would hurt and is an experience better off avoided. Now, I'm not telling you to go burn yourself or cut out your eyeballs to experience what words only describe, but experience cannot be justified through words, thoughts, memories, or assumptions. The joys and pleasures and pains of life reach through experience, such as the joy of running or the sadness of heartbreak.

What about rape? Murder? Child prostitution? Abusing the elderly? Human sacrifices? Pricking people at a nightclub with a discrete pin that's infected with AIDS? These are the things in life that, without experience, are simply rotten and evil and bad. There is no justification, or saying that "That's just the way the world is!" in light of these terrible experiences. You don't have to be raped to know that rape is a terrifying experience.

Being aware of pain and suffering without judging it does not justify the "wrongness" of these actions. Rape and murder and enticing pain and suffering does occur and it is indeed terrible, and it is important to remember that these actions only come from the weakest, most diluted, and fear-filled people around. The world is unfortunately filled with these types of people, and it isn't very nice and makes us wonder "Where is our God now!"

On the contrary, being aware of this pain and suffering without judgement does not justify these actions and allows the perpetrators to continue raping and burning the world. In fact, by looking upon a murder and pointing at it and saying "Bad," many internalise the "badness" of the situation and breed fear in their hearts. For the murderer, locking yourself away in your home with a rifle on your lap to protect you and your family from the murderer isn't going to stop the murderer from murdering someone else.

But at least you'll be safe and your fear will keep you alive.

While others continue to be hacked apart.

I have a proposition: pay attention to your mind whenever you view a situation that immediately brings the word "bad" to your mind. A lady yells at a child. Bad! A bunch of kids are kicking the four-eyed fellow at the playground. Bad! A junkie shoots up in the stall next to you, overdoses and dies. Bad! Every time that your brain injects the thought titled "Bad!" into your mind, into your awareness, change it to "Absence of fear." In some circles, the absence of Fear could be described as Love, but we'll get into that later.

Fear as a manifestation of disease

By removing the element of fear from situations judged as Bad, you are actively putting yourself into that situation through fearlessness.

When you have no fear in a situation, you are aware. In awareness, you know who you are. You exist and you are *being* in the *Now*, the moment and reality at hand. Thus, from awareness and a lack of fear you know what you'll do at any given time, and you'll do it with virtue and compassion.

You don't put yourself in a pub to not be an alcoholic.

You don't put yourself in a library to not be knowledgeable.

Through the lack of fear and a still mind, you are aware of true help, and you can put yourself in a position where people need help. With fear, many often put themselves in a position to help where people don't need help, and thus they are rendered useless.

Fear diseases the mind and exemplifies your uselessness. You hold on to memories, imaginary thoughts of the past that promote present blindness; you then project assumptions about these memories. The fear then lodges into your organs, festering and bubbling like boils, and in the end, the diseases tear you apart from your

Oneness. They incapacitate your wholeness. Memories of evil strike fear, and the fear promotes further assumptions about how an evil affects your well-being and peacefulness. Paralysed, sabotaged, and thoughts running at thousands of kilometres an hour, the fear promotes reduced sociability, exercise, nutrition, calmness, and most importantly, the fear hinders your ability to love.

Trapped and downtrodden, the "badness" and the resulting fear of judged awareness promotes a continued reality as such.

Hence: Mind is all there is.

YOU ARE REALITY.

If being aware of your reality makes you sick, watch it without judgement, follow your breath and still your mind, and you won't experience fear. Without fear you are one with yourself, and a little voice that comes from your heart. An honest and true and compassionate voice is suddenly loud enough for you to hear, and by listening to that voice, you'll know exactly what it is to be Who You Are. You'll have no other choice except to be you.

Disease. Dis-ease. A lack of ease.

When you're at ease, without tension, comfort prevails. A world full of what seems to be death and destruction certainly promotes tension, which can also be said to be a result of fear. In transition from the global destruction and problems and how you can keep yourself together and be the reality in which your still mind experiences, let's take the pains that are experienced by a much larger group of people. The pains that, perhaps, virtually everyone in the world experiences at one time or another evolve from a lack of ease. But first of all, with questions of destruction and rape, heartache, sadness, and fear, I must make one thing clear: I have no answers to the problems of the world. I cannot fix your lives. Reality is something that doesn't provide answers in the way that you and I seek resolution to the difficulties we see.

Since you are reality, the truths to the problems that you experience in life are within you and only you. A doctor cannot cure a heartache, drugs and other substances only numb heartache and wedge it deeper into your reality.

To access the truth within you, sacrifice a little time and refrain from going down the easy path.

In the face of continual sadness and heartache at a personal level, supplementing and preparing for further diseases in the mind and greater attachment and fear to worldly pleasures and stimulation, the loss of reality and the projection of yourself as simply an assumption of yourself comes down to distraction and wanting and needing newness all of the time. Naturally, new experience is one of the greatest pleasures in life.

When writing a book, many authors feel this great excitement and energy over their idea. On average, many writers finish about a third of their book when the weight of the project bears down, all of the writing and editing and work that needs to be done to continue on the idea requires far too much work. The excitement of the new idea fades, and suddenly the mind, fearful of all the work ahead, blasts the writer with a shot of stimulation and excitement right into the veins by providing a new and awesome idea! It isn't until the third of the new idea is exhausted that a new and awesome idea arises! And the cycle continues, and we are not aware, we are not in the *Now*, we are searching and searching for the same hit but off a different flavour.

With this metaphor in mind, it's easy to see that it's not the act of making love that some cherish, but the act of making love to different people all of the time. The misconceptions and illusions of relationships present an imprisonment to many, whereas they all are wanting the same stimulation but from a different body.

Fear is the one-sided manifestation of disease as it occurs within the mind. It is the discomfort and tension that transmits to all parts of our days and forms our realities. In forming our realities it forms our awareness and our illusions of the world. Fear only showcases the side of fear.

Thus, in your journey of reality and experience, I have a different proposition to replace your fear—and that is Love.

Love is not one-sided, but it is all around and wraps all of the "good" and "bad" that the world presents in odd ways. Love smiles in the same language and knows no scales. Scales may give you balance—yet love has no measurement on either side. Love smiles in the same language wherever you go.

Love is the eternal gratefulness of the *Now*, and the reality and truth that you have uncovered within yourself. Through the replacement of fear from your life with Love, you can *be*. You are Who You Are. There is no responding to memories in the past or worrying about the future when you have Love in your every moment.

Thus, in the face of fear and death and destruction in the world, you can still your mind, eliminate the fear, and experience the role that Love plays in the reality that is *You*.

Fear and Love. Death and Life. The duality of the universe.

Your true self experienced through your no self.

Which brings us to The Tao.

Chapter 3

The Tao (The Way)

Love

'Embracing Tao, you become embraced.

Supple, breathing gently, you become reborn.

Clearing your vision, you become clear.

Nurturing your beloved, you become impartial.

Opening your heart, you become accepted.

Accepting the World, you embrace Tao.

Bearing and nurturing,

Creating but not owning,

Giving without demanding,

Controlling without authority,

This is love.

—Lao Tzu

Getting into the seriousness of why it is that life stretches its existential hands in all directions, touching each and every one of us in the form of punches to the eye or soft caresses along the back of the head, is certainly a serious matter. We are loved one minute, and in the next, we are shattered, broken, and destitute. The rich eventually fall. The beautiful love suddenly ends. The criminals and the evil stand on the top of the hill while the good hold the weight of the hill on their shoulders. There's a devil on one shoulder and an angel on the other. Heaven above and Hell below. Life starts just to eventually introduce us to death. We smile and frown. Cry and laugh. Reflect the most beautiful and the most horrifying in the same expression of the eyes. We are all left-brained and right-brained. Creativity and organisation. Large and small. Without one we have no clue what would be the other.

And in the midst of the chaos, the exposition of the light contrasted against the dark, we have those who watch without judgement, who take the weight of fear off their shoulders and experience *being* in the *Now*.

In the simplest mode possible, the Tao is simply The Way, and without diving into a history and geographical lesson of how the Tao came to be the way it is today with the writings and reflections of Lao Tzu and the growth of

Taoism as a way of life, that's all that you need to know for now.

The Tao is The Way

Let's further our confusion, shall we?

At this very moment, I would like you to imagine nothing. Try to picture in your mind what nothing would be. If you are like me and everyone else, we imagine nothing as simply this blank space, probably all black or all white. However, black and white are colours. In terms of nothing, we are without colour, without space or time. Nothingness can never be "this," and it can never be "that." Nothingness has no name, for if it had a name it would then be something. In fact, trying to think of "nothing" is in itself an act of creation, as you are then projecting your idea of what nothing would look like to you. Thus, to understand Tao, it is crucial to remember that our brains, as great and complex as they are, are still quite limited nonetheless; the brain is incapable of constructing what would be absolute nothingness, and in a way, this is Tao.

When you have become Who You Are, without judgements, plans, or expectations, you become the Way. In a different presentation, when you are simply yourself, with nothing more except for your essence, you are then Truth. Your essence is reality, and when reality is you, you are so in the moment at every point in your life that you no longer wake up with anxiety, your experience of seriousness and work turns out to be fun and enjoyment. You uphold no fear. Balance and simplicity ring true throughout your every movement.

Cultivation of a quiet mind and calm heart

Through stillness, a quiet mind, and a calm heart, you can discover an incredible joy that many cover entire continents to find: simplicity, compassion, tolerance, serenity, and most importantly, love everything you do and all that you are. This is the Tao, and no matter what has happened in your past or what type of person you believe yourself to be, the Tao solely serves to bring you back to the basics and eliminates the illusion of confusion and struggle from life.

Like the dirty window mentioned in Chapter 1, Tao is a window cleaner. Taoism is not a religion but maybe practices similar to a religion and in some countries may be considered as such. What I am and talking about is not a religion nonetheless and requires no conversion from your current beliefs or religious practices. There are no rituals that you must conduct, no goats to slay. There is no Nirvana or Heaven to reach; there is no Hell to fight against. Nirvana and Heaven is your life and your *Now*. Unlike other "isms," Taoism is simply a way of life that promotes virtue, discipline, compassion, and simplicity.

Taoism is The Way to eliminate excess, sensual desire, commercialism, hatred, and the infinite fear. Within the Tao, there is no separation and thus there is no attachment.

"When there is no more separation of this and that—this is called the still point of the Tao"

—Monk Xu

We are all part of conflict & duality, of Love & Fear but these are only two parts still connected to the same whole.

Simplicity and Effortlessness

If the Tao could be anything at all, it would be simplicity and effortless all in one package. There are no documents or books that describe the role of Tao to save humanity from the evils of suffering and sin. Although we can trace Taoism to the book, the Tao Te Ching, written around the 6th century BC by the sage, Lao Tzu, the Tao Te Ching is really simply a manual, a collection of 81 poems to showcase a way to live through the absence of power and the practice of virtue. However, through the Tao Te Ching, you will get to value the three treasures although reaching Nirvana is not the goal, and in essence, the only practice Taoism emphasises is letting go—that is watching the breath to simply let it go.

Breathe in and fill your lungs, watch the breath enter, and then slowly, being aware the entire time, breathe out. This focus on your breath gives your brain no place to go, and you are no longer a program that follows a pre-organised plan. When your brain has no place to go as you watch your breath, you simply go with the *Flow*.

Taoism is the truth in your awareness which sincerely watches. Focus on the moment, exist and be Who You Are, embrace simplicity, and by all means, let go. That is The Way to a peaceful and focused life, a cultivated spirit capable of seeing the world clearly.

But it all sounds good and dandy on the surface, and while in meditation you can be the most peaceful, calm, and focused person there is. Around other people following The Way with discipline and sincerity, you may find it more difficult to follow your breath, exist in the *Now*, and watch your thoughts without judgement. However, the challenge comes when you out of meditation and joining in with the frightening speeds of life, complete with fast cars honking for seemingly no purpose but just to make noise and exert dominance, people scrambling to work and choking down coffee and cigarettes, hatred and fear, social anxiety, a million tasks to do, overwhelming hours ticking away the moments of the day until you are up at night, lying in bed, with all of your thoughts and worries placing themselves within your consciousness so that you can't even sleep.

Staying on the path, on The Way, is not easy in this world.

But when looking to compound your life with simplicity in Love, just remember: Don't Worry. It's not easy and that's okay, and sometimes the more difficult path can present pleasures and new experiences that scare and excite at the same time.

Thus, as you are presented with every moment of your day, every *Now* that you try to focus upon, remember two crucially important words:

1. Virtue
2. Sincerity

Repeat these words over and over again when you find yourself in a difficult situation, and in the face of challenges, challenge yourself with Love in your heart. Utilise discipline to experience the infinite, and for every thought you have, word you speak, and action you conduct, do it in sincerity. In respect to simplicity, a Taoist Monk is just that: Virtuousness and Sincerity.

Use these two modes in your actions, and when on the path to existing as Who You Are, living in the *Now*, you have three stages to enlightenment:

1. Self-realisation
2. Actualisation
3. Embodiment

As stated earlier, it is quite impossible and useless to try and imagine nothingness, but in the duality of the Tao, the nothingness is understood through the 'union of all things'.

Nothingness is everything. Hence, understanding the self, the Who You Are, can only be accomplished by understanding that there is no-self therefore no ego.

By being *Reality*, you are the *Essence* in everything. By being the *Essence* in everything, there is no separation, and therefore no attachment

Once the no-self realises that it is an ocean, you can easily see that in the ocean, everything is right where it needs to be. The universe is as it is, and it is nothing more.

Therefore, as most of the things in life need to be experienced and cannot be explained, the no-self realises that there is no such thing as death, and only through death can you understand what this phenomenon means.

Why be afraid of death? Is your life such procrastination that Death is going to be the thing to stop you from living? It's coming anyway, so live in the *Now* and *Flow*.

Self-realisation, the no-self, all comes down to simplicity and living without meanings, definitions, and expectations. You let the mind become still and listen to that inner voice, and you experience the outside world with utmost attention. Through this understanding and disciplined daily practice, the no-self also promotes actualisation, practice.

And in terms of actualisation, or practicing the Tao and the inner voice as you have understood it, is as simple as *being* in the moment, the *Now*. Practice comes with no set expectations, absolutely nothing at all, and therefore, you can't put the no-self into practice if you are expecting to receive enlightenment. Therefore following Taoism just for the sake of fulfilling your dreams is like following a homeless man for a home to sleep in. You won't find it or it is not yours to begin with. You have to be in the moment and be content in not knowing what is around the corner because...

Being in the moment basically means: *Not knowing what is going to happen!*

Through being by not knowing, living in the *Now*, and by being Who You Are, you have already taken the last step towards both emptying and filling your mind, and that is the embodiment of going beyond realisations and being The Way.

Being still, quieten the mind and be aware of your inner and outer experiences, all of this is being The Way, and living in the Tao and in the *Now* because

Now is All There Really Is.

Chapter 4

Sufism and the Mystery of Life

There are two aspects of individual harmony: the harmony between body and soul, and the harmony between individuals. All the tragedy in the world, in the individual and in the multitude, comes from lack of harmony. And harmony is the best given by producing harmony in one's own life.

—Hazrat Inayat Khan

Islam.

What is the first thing that comes to your mind on this word? What is the first image or set of dialogue that judges, describes, or gives breath to this religion? For Muslims, Islam is the voluntary submission to God and the way in life in service to God. For several non-Muslims, in this day and age of media-sponsored Fear and the seemingly constant onslaught that seems to come from the more hard-lined branches of Islam, the word presents terrorism, war, beheadings, the subjugation of women, and other unpleasantness. For even yet other non-Muslims, Islam is just another religion, which caters to hundreds of millions of peaceful, normal folk just like you and I, trying to make ends meet in struggles they are presented with.

Discipline, serenity, and mindfulness

Within the Islamic sphere of belief, we can find yet another branch that experiences life in a much different sphere, whereas many of the concepts of Taoism and the importance of discipline, serenity, and mindfulness are present, and that branch is Sufism.

In a nutshell, Sufism is the Truth and the selfless experience and actualisation of the Truth through means of love and devotion. Much like the emptying of the mind and the casting of the ego, Sufism revolves around an enlightened inner being without the shackles of logic, revelation, or intellectual proof. Through the clear vision of the inner being, which can only be realised through the quiet and stillness of the mind, the entirety of Reality can be perceived.

Thus, you can imagine why Sufism is included in this book, and to think of it clearly, we have a likeness between the sphere of light metaphor from the last chapter and this following metaphor that utilises the image of the ocean:

If we were to associate the Whole, the *Now* and the reality, to be as an Ocean, and if part of the whole would be likened to a drop, then the Sufis say that to witness this entire Ocean with the eyes contained in a drop of water would be impossible. This isn't so hard to imagine, as jumping into the middle of the ocean truly only allows a miniscule portion of the entire Earth to be seen. However, when the drop becomes one with the Ocean, just as you becoming *one* with Reality and being Who You Are, you are able to see the entire Ocean with the eye of the mind.

An ancient tale promotes this idea that Monk Xu has been detailing throughout this book and my pleasant chats with him throughout the past couple weeks, and in fact, the idea comes from one of the most famous and everlasting Sufi mystics there are: Jalal ad-Din Muhammad Rumi, or also known simply as, Rumi. His story goes as follows:

This story revolves around a group of men who had never, not once in their lives, seen an elephant before. Then, one day out of the blue, amidst complete darkness around them, they came upon an elephant. Once again, it was complete darkness and nobody could see a thing when they approached the animal, but each man resulted in feeling a part of the elephant to get an idea of what an elephant was. Afterwards, they all gathered around to describe what they thought that had perceived.

The one man who felt the elephant's leg imagined the creature to resemble a pillar. The one who felt the ear described the elephant as a giant fan. Each one of their descriptions regarding the various parts of the elephant that they had experienced was absolutely true, but when describing the elephant in its entirety, they had fallen short. Thus, if only one of them had a candle to illuminate that darkness, their different opinions would not have came forth. Instead, the candle would have revealed the elephant as a Whole.

In this story, and in Sufism, and in Taoism, and in listening to your inner voice and quieting the confusion and stress that comes from a diseased mind, we have a light that serves as a path, a Way, where the Truth can be discovered.

Yes, Sufism is a branch of Islam, and even within Islam, we find parallels towards the ideas of Oneness and the revelation of Truth in its entirety that comes from being One with Reality. No matter the "ism," all of this relates to the quiet and still mind, the dedication, discipline, and sincerity towards all of your actions, and the Love that you are as opposed to confounding your life with perceptions, assumptions, and Fear.

Whirling Dervishes

However, Sufism has always been an interesting way of thought, as from Sufism we can truly gather some very insightful and exceedingly beautiful ideas that help us understand and realise this world a little more clearly. One way in particular, and a beautiful vision that Monk Xu often referred to, was that of the Sufi Whirling dances often conducted by a Sufi Dervish, or one who follows an ascetic path of extreme poverty and austerity. These dances have been made quite famous worldwide from countries such as Turkey, as for many it serves as a tourist attraction.

But from within the dances, this whirling has a much more profound significance, being a physically active meditation within the *Sema*, or religious ceremony. It is through this dance where the dancer has one hand pointed skyward—*receiving from above, within*—and the other hand pointed downward—*giving back to the Earth, outside.* If you were given the grace to witness such an event, you would see a handful of dancers wearing colourful cloaks tied at the waist, allowing the lower half of the robe to flow outwards and twirl with the dancer. Their arms are extended parallel to the ground, with the fingers of one hand cupped upwards and the other downwards. The upwards hand is the listening, the receiving, of the universe, the *Flow* and the *Now*, the little voice within, the Heavens from above, the Who You Are, while the hand pointing downwards is the Reality that you live in, and the discipline, virtue, sincerity, and actualisation of the *Now*, the giving back to the Earth.

The dancer revolves around and around and, as it is in Sufism, everything is revolving. There is no end point or beginning, just as your life has no end or beginning, it simply *is*. You are the *Flow* that you see in the world, and being in unison transmits the energy from above, into you, and through you the energy is creation in what you give back to the world.

There is no outwardly message that delineates Who You Are; you are not waiting for a sign from God or Nature, as by making your life a series of waiting, you become just that, a waiter.

The Sufi Whirling Dervishes spin and spin, their eyes closed with every muscle in their faces relaxed, meditation through movement, and the mind is solidified in stillness, the tension releases; the ecstasy of the moment brings the Dervishes within, and they can hear the voices of their own bodies and souls without illusions and rationalisations created by the brain and visualised in the mind. The act brings them to source.

"Whatever is in the heavens and whatever is on the earth is exalting Allah to him belongs dominions and to Him belongs all praise and He is over all things competent."

—Qur'ān, 64:1

Whatever you see, things that are deemed as "good" or "bad," is of a Godly nature.

It's all perfection, including you, and a vision within, clear and un-muddied, reveals the Truth of Who You Are, and who you are meant to be. Life is meant for gratitude of the experience, and not for casting away the evils you see within yourself or in the world outside.

Look upon the evils and illusions that you create, and through the loss of ego, the no-self, you too are upon the perfection of the world that just is, of you just *being*, existing through your spirit, body, and mind, together.

When your gratefulness for the way the world is, the Way You Are, envelopes all that is around you, you can see and feel that there is nothing more you'd want from it. You'd let go of the idea of more and embrace what is.

Will a red sports car express Who You Are, as a person and part of Nature? Does this car provide the experience of a "better" life when you are life?

Does a job you hate, with prerequisites of eight hours a day in loneliness amidst a team-player atmosphere, showcase your gratefulness for family, friends, food, and Love?

Although Sufism revels in minimalism with sages of old in extreme poverty, it does not mean that you need to cast away all of your worldly possessions, quit your job, and embrace absolute nothingness as you imagine it. Instead, look around you, be grateful for what you have, still the mind, and end the attachment you have to the things you think you own; it is the only Way to also end the Fear of separation from everything around you.

Through Sufism, we also acquire a picture of what the mystery of life could be, and the solutions to it all.

And there is no mystery, no secret code or loophole in the Matrix. The secret is that the world is going to continue to do what it is doing, and through true Love of both yourself and the world, and the realisation that both are of the same, that which comes from within then expresses itself on Earth in the form of creation.

One hand upwards revealing the spirit within, and one hand downwards, flowing through you and revolving, revolving, revolving, and it's you giving to the Earth, your creation.

Furthermore, even in Sufism we have no programs, no specific ways to act to receive grace and discover the creative attributes within you. You are not a piece of cattle, a worker, a follower, nor a leader. You just are. And you evolve just like the Whirling Dervishes. Through realisation of Love for all beings and gratefulness of everything around you, through your discipline and sincerity on what your heart is saying, life then becomes a service to others and the world around you.

Cast away the ego, the ideas of popularity and your assumptions of a good life that material items will bring, and you are only left with pure creativity, of Love.

Islam, Christianity, Buddhism, Judaism, Wicca, Atheism, and all of the other ways of life and beliefs that we form, most come down with being the person that you are, listening to your soul and experiencing Love in all of its forms. If Love is in everything, then your everyday life is Love.

Although many of these ways of life seek to say that our Reality is Hell, that life is death and destruction and evil, that confusion and depression are ubiquitous, and that only through devotion and worship, a program to follow, serves to provide you access to something that is "better," through Love revolving within and without, the miracle of creation that is this Universe is also within you.

Hafiz, is a great Sufi poet from the 1300's whose intoxicating poetry talking about oneness with the Creator. Hafiz, along with many Sufi masters spoke about hypocrisy and deceit that exists in society and was outspoken about this. His works are testament of the Sufi culture and clear expressions of his love for the Divine.

As Whirling Dervishes represent, receive from above; be grateful for all that there is because it is all a miracle. Many forget, about things so commonplace as miracles blend right into their surroundings.

But with a hand up, a hand down, a quiet mind and the connection of the within and the without, a drop of water that is one with the Ocean and can see it all, a candle in the darkness so the whole elephant can be seen, it is the Truth of life that we experience, and it is the You that You Are. Escape confusion, consumerism, and death, separation and attachment.

For you are Life. You live on a rock that "peopled," just as an apple tree apples.

You want to see a miracle that solves your mystery? Look at yourself and see Who You Are within.

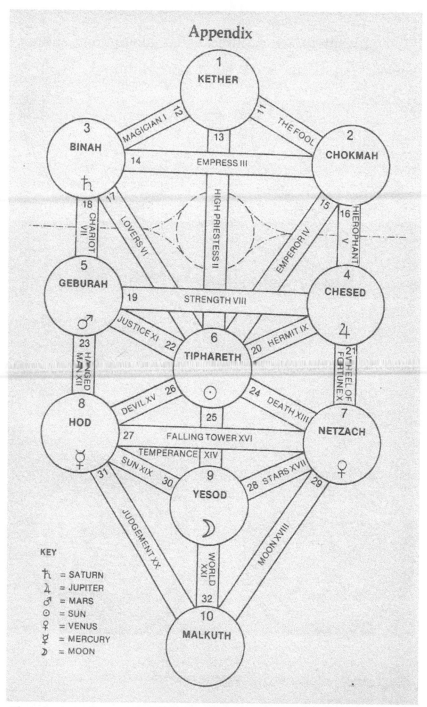

Appendix

Photo Courtesy of Loga, J. (1986). *The Prediction Book of Amulets and Talisman*, p. 117

Chapter 5

The Kabbalah
(Wisdom of the Tree of Life)

With each experience we grow and become more aware of the inner beauty that lies within us. Ultimately we are truly our own leader. We lead the connection and flow of life that is our inheritance.

—Rabbi Yossi

Taoism, Sufism, and the Kabbalah: the three schools that have given enlightenment in this world, exposing the universe within you and the inner voice that must be listened to and not discarded for the assumptions and projections that the mind presents. Furthering in this section of the book, and expanding upon the Mind and the *Now*, Monk Xu and I dived deeper into the global acknowledgement of what it means to be alive, spanning religions, time, and space. Overcoming the ego and setting aside religious belief. Know that you don't need to even believe in a God to realise that within you, you have all of the answers that you ever needed in Life, to be the person you are without any second guessing.

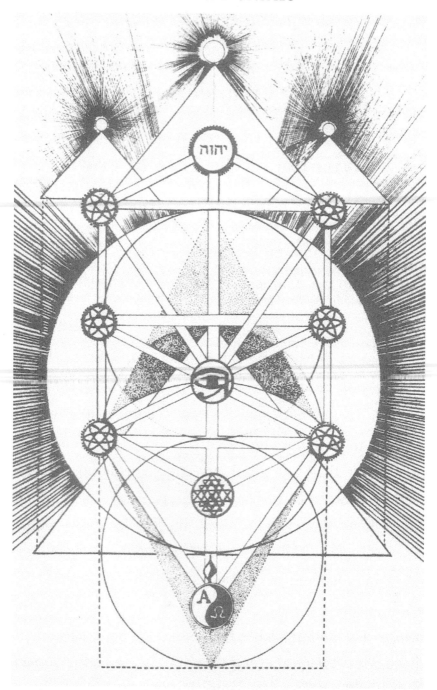

Photo Courtesy of Hurtak, J. (1997). *An Introduction to the Keys of Enoch.* p. 92

In Taoism, we are given the idea of duality, the existence of the world and our own existence in it, and that nothing is "good" or "bad," as they just *are* and provide definitions for the other. In Sufism, we explored the idea that life revolves, it has no beginning or end as there is no attachment or separation.

If E=MC2, whereas energy is equal to mass times the speed of light, squared, then on the other side of the coin, all of the energy that was ever used can be converted back into matter, bound by space and time, and matter back into energy. In Kabbalah, we then have the wisdom that ties it all together, inserts more sense in the topics that Monk Xu is presenting, so that we can turn our realisation of the Truth into practice and embodiment, by far the most difficult aspect of it all.

Kabbalah, literally meaning "to receive" is basically an esoteric method, discipline, and school of thought that dates back to antiquity Judaism, in the time where the Jewish peoples were cast from Israel to Babylon, and it serves as the mystic roots and wisdom that provide practical tools to create (not achieve), joy and lasting fulfilment. In the words of the Kabbalist Yehuda Ashlag, The Essence of the Wisdom of Kabbalah" is:

"This wisdom in no more and no less than a sequence of roots, which hang down by way of cause and effect, in fixed, determined rules, interweaving in a single, exalted goal described as, 'the revelation of His Godliness to His Creatures in this world.'"

You don't need to believe in a God, and by no means are we trying to convert you to Taoism, Islam, or Judaism, but the point of these inclusions remains: the Life that You Are, the miracle, is an integral part of the creation of the universe.

You do matter! You are matter! (Quite literally...)

Without assumptions, plans, or ideas about the Reality around you, you see that the perfection of duality is everywhere, that everything is a miracle. Thus, in fearlessness, in Love, the no attachment and no separation, the "bad" that gives life to the "good," it is all examples of perfect Love.

You don't need to believe in a God, but isn't perfect Love the ideal description of God?

Timeless Wisdom from the Ten Sefirot

Just as it is in the duality, where Love is understood through Fear and the self is understood through the no-self, the wisdom of Kabbalah can also be understood with reference to what it is not. Therefore, Kabbalah is not what we can easily imagine in our minds—it is an infinite, a no-end. The true essence of God, Nature, You, is known as the Ein Sof, literally translating to "without end." There are no boundaries in time and space, and it has no interaction with the universe, as it is one with the universe. Both female and male, the Kabbalah and the Ein Sof does present a small degree of interaction with the universe, corresponding to the qualities of God and Reality, of which we create and express in our daily lives and our mental capacity of the experience of finite reality, known as the Ten Sefirot.

The Ten Sefirot are as follows:

1. Keter (The Crown)
2. Chokhmah (Wisdom)
3. Binah (Intuition, Understanding)
4. Chesed or Gedulah (Loving Kindness)
5. Gevurah (Strength)
6. Tiferet (Beauty)
7. Netzach (Victory)
8. Hod (Acknowledgement)
9. Yesod (Foundation)
10. Malkut (Kingdom)

The Crown describes the Divine Will above intellect and all else, including reason, assumption, and logic. You don't need to believe in God to know that a voice inside of you translates Who You Are, and it is this Divine Will that expresses the Reality around you. Quiet the mind, follow your breath, be still, and without intellect or consciousness, you can experience Reality and Truth of the being, the *Now*.

However, the Divine Will, Nature, *Now*, or whatever words you want to describe this, does require a bit of intellect as well in regards to self-realisation, the first step to enlightenment. Wisdom, or Divine Intellect, is basically you being aware of your own Divine Will. It is the awareness and the non-judgemental view of the world around you, and it is you putting yourself in a position to help where you are useful, where you are of service to yourself and others. The Divine Intellect is the casting away of Fear, and the expression of Love, or the Way You Are.

Lastly, the latter Sefirot express the conscious Divine Emotions, or the soul that is mirroring the Divine. But it is not so much in the ordering as in the construction of the Sefirot where we experience a more profound configuration of our understanding of finite reality. Keep in mind that the relationship of the Ten Sefirot are neither separate or attachment, but instead, connected through a network of channels (tzinorot) that showcase the *Flow* of energy.

Basically, the Ten Sefirot are divided into three triplets of three, consisting of right, left, and middle at three different levels. The first triplet, The Crown, Wisdom, and Understanding, is known as the triplet of the Mind. The second triplet, Loving Kindness, Strength, and Beauty, is the inner emotive powers that your heart expresses before you begin to act or do things. The third triplet, Victory, Acknowledgement, Foundation, is of action by means of behaviouristic characteristics. Although the third triplet consists of emotions, it is important to remember that these emotions only manifest through behaviour.

If you are anything like me in math, it took me a while to realise that we forgot the last one: Kingdom. This final point can either be an appendage or an independent entity that receives all of the collected energy from the Sefirot preceding it, but in all, Kingdom (or Reality, or the *Now*), is the final result of all the experiences of the soul.

Thus, we have three triplets that all, connected but not attached, provide our Kingdom, our *Now*, just as the many other "threes" in the Universe do: past, present, and future are all one that determines our life at this moment in space and time. Super-conscious, conscious, and subconscious all exist to determine our mind. Two straight lines cannot possibly enclose any space or form a plane figure, just as two plane surfaces cannot form a solid; instead, three lines, three dimensions form the length, breadth, and height to form a solid; three stands for solid, real, substantial, complete, and entire. Thought, word, and deed sum up human capability. Three is God's attributes: Omniscience, omnipresence, and omnipotence.

All of it comes down, *Flows*, into our Kingdom, our present, our Reality, our *Now*.

A Tool for Clarity and Knowing

Are we putting the connections together? If not, Monk Xu speaks softly and sincerely, like a Lion that devours its prey with Love and with the existence of Nature, and often I find myself full of assumptions, and Fears, and confusion, like a Lion afraid of looking stupid in the presence of bigger, stronger Lions. He laughs, just as confused and full of assumptions as I am, and says that it is only discipline and sincerity, in the Tao or the Way, the Sufi Dervishes, and the Ein Sof, that the "no end," the "no-self," is envisioned and embodied. By no means is it exclusive. And he concludes the revolving door or self-realisation through the wisdom of Kabbalah.

In the end of all that we've talked about thus far, the *Flow* and the *Now*, the descending Divinity that produces the kingdom of our lives, and the stillness of the mind to discover the inner light and to cast away illusions, is that in this midst of all this great sounding stuff, perfect Love spread across the world and the upbringing of Fearlessness, is that we all have free will.

Basically, we are capable of doing whatever we would like.

We can turn from all directives, from the inner light and voice beneath the ramblings in the mind, and give into an attachment of desires that aren't in line with our true selves. On the other hand, our free will also puts us in a partnership with God in Creation.

Anything that you imagine, that you feel from within you and as an essence of Who You Are, is yours for Creation. God, Nature, Reality, a Higher Power of some sort, all of this cannot exist without its counterpart; in other words, if God is all there is, how does God know itself. Our actions, every small action that you take on an everyday basis, based on free will and choice, ripple from the physical world into the spiritual world, thus allowing the spiritual world to experience itself.

We are the Universe experiencing itself.

We are Nature experiencing itself.

We are Creation to no end.

Things we consider to be "good" or "bad," is nothing more than the experiences of the Universe, watched objectively and without bias. If there were a set of rules that would dictate our lives, then in the end it would be the

Universe forming some sort of study on us, utilising a hypothesis to reach some sort of conclusion or Law about humanity. There is no hypothesis, only experience and Creation, and the Kabbalah is just one of the many modes of thought that dive into this realisation. And according to the Kabbalah, everything on this Earth, being a being of creation from a Creator, that provides a message of any sorts, is an Angel.

Angels do the will of its Creator following their inner voice and acknowledging the *Now*. However, humanity are not like Angels, as we have free will to do or not do what it is we feel is in our souls. We can choose to take a nap instead of going to the local soup kitchen to volunteer. We can choose to watch television instead of writing that book or building that design you imagined. Gravity, on the other hand, just does what it is supposed to do. In the same light, your angel, your will, can be accessed by being Who You Are. And in the Kabbalah we encounter a very similar parallel to Sufism, whereas our free will is influenced by two cycles: one from the side of angels, and the other from the side of humans.

We have the voice inside of you that can be heard with a still mind, the Way You Are the angel within you *receiving from above*. But still, what occurs on Earth, results of our free will, is still energy that reaches the above, and if there is no harmony, you can find no peace, no simplicity, no Truth or perfect Love.

We are the Dervish whirlers, receiving from above and giving to Earth, and in the middle, it all revolves and revolves and revolves.

Seek the harmony between what you receive and what you give, and thus you exist just as you are. When you are Who You Are, there is nothing more you need, want, or desire, and instead, you grateful for every single piece of Love on this planet.

You breathe and in that breath alone love resides. Fear is a shadow. The Being is responsible for all actions and all actions has a great ripple effect. They say that the wings moving from a butterfly in Brazil can create hurricanes on the other side of the world. That is how interconnected we all really are.

Chapter 6

The Tao of Addiction

Do you really want to be happy? You can begin by being appreciative of who you are and what you've got.

—Benjamin Hoff

Escaping the misery and suffering of life

All of this Who You Are, Truth, perfect Love, receiving from above and whirling Dervishes, all of these Proper Nouns and *italics* and quotes in **bold letters**, and all of these revolving sentences that blend the lines of imagination and the unimaginable, does sound quite nice when you put it in the framework of:

Be the person you feel you are, listen to your instincts, and dedicate your life to Love.

But when it comes down to the actual practice, the evolution from the old and into the new, whereas your life is defined by the things you do at every moment as opposed to the illusions that you give yourself and the wants that you desire that hang off in the future and the past, a billion trillion cool words and sentences don't mean anything. Just as the Tao cannot be explained through words, just like the candle can be described, you only truly experience through action. You only know the fire burning your skin by holding your hand over the candle; otherwise, you just have assumptions and thoughts.

And that is why drug or alcohol addiction, gambling addiction, sex addiction, and any other addiction, feels so awesomely great. Because when you're stoned or in the *zone*, man, you are also in the *Now*.

Yes.

You read that right, and no, neither Monk Xu nor I are trying to advocate addiction. Quite the contrary, actually. Let's begin.

Life as many of us know it travels at thousands of kilometres an hour, and its filled with all of these obligations, structures, programs, and things that we are supposed to do to live *a good life*. Be it the American Dream, lifestyles of riches, fame, popularity; lifestyles of peace and tranquillity, lifestyles of dreams and hopes and wishes, lifestyles of assumptions and prepositions, none of it feels right at the moment for some of us, be we prevail anyways in hopes of the little gift baggy waiting at the end of the line. That success. That feeling of "By gum and my grandma's hat, I've done it!"

"I'm here! I've made it to the top and only had to cut a few throats along the way."

And then, now what? You're 50 years old, you've followed the structure that you were told by society is right, and now you've lived through five decades. So you buy a new car, a boat, sleep with younger women or men, go off and be crazy because you've lost so many years putting off pleasure in regards to work. You buy the sofa because it is the last sofa you will ever need.

One of my preferred monologues that detail the scope of life, as many of us know it, comes from the book/movie Trainspotting, and it goes a bit like this:

"Choose Life. Choose a job. Choose a career. Choose a family. Choose a fucking big television, choose washing machines, cars, compact disc players and electrical tin openers. Choose good health, low cholesterol, and dental insurance. Choose fixed interest mortgage repayments. Choose a starter home. Choose your friends. Choose leisurewear and matching luggage. Choose a three-piece suit on hire purchase in a range of fucking fabrics. Choose DIY and wondering who the fuck you are on Sunday morning. Choose sitting on that couch watching mind-numbing, spirit-crushing game shows, stuffing fucking junk food into your mouth. Choose rotting away at the end

of it all, pissing your last in a miserable home, nothing more than an embarrassment to the selfish, fucked up brats you spawned to replace yourselves. Choose your future. Choose life... But why would I want to do a thing like that? I chose not to choose life. I chose somethin' else. And the reasons? There are no reasons. Who needs reasons when you've got heroin?"

—**Irvine Welsh, *Trainspotting***

Insatiable desire for destruction

Surely, we are not all like the character depicted in Irvine Welsh's book, whereas the reality of life is bleak and we are a doomed species just waiting to escape from our miserable lives, but the essence is there in the illusions that we dictate to form a "good" life. The essence in addiction, heroin, gambling, or any other, is that it allows us not to be a part of the consumerist society, the jobs we hate and the things that don't feel right in our hearts. There is no focus on Nature, on gravity, on receiving from within and giving back to the Earth; no desire to still the mind, watch the world without judgement, and be the Way You Are while experiencing the world just as it is.

In addiction however, we can escape the misery and sufferings of life, the Calvin Klein underwear and fake smiles to mask the dullness and boredom, the stress from bills and waking up every morning not believing that you are about to head to the office for another full day of sitting on a chair and feeling your butt get sore, anxiously watching the clock, making the clock your God, for a coffee break, a cigarette break, a holiday, and so on.

I've met thousands of different people while travelling, and so has Monk Xu, and one of the strangest things we've heard, that we agree upon, is how at the end of a holiday, the common phrase is: "Well, back to reality." As if the holiday wasn't reality, but a dream or an imagined escape from the reality that you created in the first place.

Thus, whenever the card dealer is flipping that last card, you have two aces in your hand and $25,000 on the table, whenever that bloody rose shoots up into your syringe, signifying that you've hit the vein and are ready for take-off, whenever you look down at your cell phone and the buttons resemble the controls of a spaceship, the acid taking hold, the struggles and seemingly pointless nature of life don't matter one bit anymore. You lose all of the stress that you have been building, and all of a sudden the colours are brighter, your scents are "on" like the Lion moving in for the kill, everything is sharp, and all of a sudden, there is Love and excitement in everything.

Then, when you are addicted to your substance or behaviour, the only worry and anxiety and stress that you have revolves around filling your need, and the rest takes a backseat.

But things aren't simple, there is no virtue or giving back to the Earth, and by all means, your mind isn't still and you need, need, need, and need some more. There is never enough, and the high always goes away, the perfect Love and the Way always fades. The only discipline you have is how hard you work to get your fix, and the only sincerity you cater is for how much you need your addiction.

There's no respect, especially for your body and peace of mind, and you're aware that your addiction is a problem before even coming into it. Furthermore, you're tightly attached, and when there is attachment, there is Fear in separation. Life is Fear in this sense. As you're body tells you otherwise, tells you of the Way and the Truth of Who You Are, you lie to yourself, your brain produces all of these thoughts based on the survival of the dopamine rush, the serenity that you think you need to maintain, and you sabotage everything.

You feel the *Now* when you're high, and you're able to experience this sincere awareness of your surroundings, in the zone, but there is no oneness, as your heart and your body tells you otherwise, and you lie and fill your life with illusions, and within you, a great struggle revolves around and around.

As an addict, you are a Dervish whirler, but your dance looks more like a seizure than anything.

Being in the den of addiction, being constantly drug induced, nothing that comes out of an addict's mouth makes any sense, and the explanations are like hearing fairy tales or a hoax. It's them, the addicts, staying in one spot being beaten on a path of self-destruction. You can't escape the Reality that you are in, nor can you escape Who You Are. But you can deny these things and fill your mind with all sorts of creative illusions.

Moreover, your mind is never closed, 24/7 it stays open; it's infinite and nothingness at the same time, and you can never close nothingness.

Between the programs of reality, the dental insurance and low cholesterol pills, three-piece suits and getting quite drunk every Friday and Saturday night, and the option of addiction to escape the dullness that you imagine you see, that you are almost trained to see in the program of life, there is a third way out (or in, as I like to think of it).

For the soul's true journey to flower, all things need to be given up. There must be no attachment, no need, and you'll find no fear of separation. It all comes down to Love and Fearlessness, and the cycle of addiction is simply one based on Fear and cowardice. Fear instigates a lack of awareness, as you become bent on your illusions that you need your addictions to maintain in Reality, to accomplish different concepts that you have for yourself.

But a further problem arises in drug abuse and addiction, and that is the altered reality that you create from the abuse that you give your mind, the slowed wits and the actual damages and changes that extensive abuse can elicit. Your thought patterns alter, it reaches your mind, and the confusion and distortion is enhanced to great levels, thus, if you are still in the throes of addiction, practicing the stillness and peace measured throughout this book will be impossible. The Tao of addiction is fully realised once you and your body are cleansed from intoxicants, as it is the practice and embodiment of your virtues, the Who You Are that ends the separation and attachment, and fully exposes the beauty both within and without.

The desire, the endless want and need, the continual drive for stimulation, something that both takes you away and immerses you in the *Now*, while at the same time disregarding the Reality that you feel within yourself, is not "bad" in the sense of the word. By no means does an addiction make you a bad person that needs to change to function in society. Instead, addiction cultivates the Fear and darkens the Love of the world; it puts you in a stalemate. Nothing moves forward, nothing moves backwards, and you don't have the no-self; the ego is hungry for the way you feel and look about yourself, and the hierarchy of superiority and inferiority takes hold of your life, spins it about and drives it in every which way.

To reach the peace, to cultivate focus and strength, to be the Lion who hunts, to be the Gravity that keeps everything in its place, the River that *Flows*, the *Now* that is everything and nothing at the same time, the Love in every aspect of your life, and all of your dreams fulfilled with nothing left to do before death except to experience death in all of its wonder, is not possible through addiction.

"Addiction is Fear."

—Monk Xu

And the solution is simple: get clean, breathe, balance, meditate, and listen and cultivate your spirit, all of which will be discussed in the last four chapters of this book.

You are all that there is.

You are everything and you are Love. Contrary to what you were led to believe, you are not a junkie, an addict, or a worthless human being. And if you question any of this, look deep within and still the mind, and from a still mind, your thoughts, words, and deeds can become aligned, harmonious, and peaceful.

Chapter 7

The Tao of Mental Illness

One must still have chaos in oneself to be able to give birth to a dancing star.

—Friedrich Nietzsche

Be Who You Are, there is nothing or nobody else that you can be.

You can only be You, but you are not mental illness, and to be You, it all comes down to Love.

Fear Only Makes You Lose Your Way

You can feel impressed and inspired by the actors and actresses you see in movies, who always know the right things to say, who live through the experiences that you could only wish for, and whose beauty and grace makes you wonder why you can't be that way. Surely, after the film is over, you may feel the attributes of the actors or actresses, the storylines, on your shoulders as if you were wearing a sweater, but it wears off, typically after you wake up the next morning.

The reality around you is the inner mirror of who you really are. Descriptions takes place with the utterance of thought—therefore realign the dialogue and speak truth sincerely to create a very beautiful reality around you, seeing beauty in all things.

You are only You, and to accept the Self is to accept the entire Reality around you. Gone are the days of the excuses, the lies, and the illusions you may have when it is You in the centre of your experience of the *Now*. For if the *Now* is all there is, then You can only be You.

But that brings up an interesting question, one that I have asked many, many times. As a lifelong harbourer of a bipolar disorder with ten different trips to the psychiatric hospital, a few 'shocking' electroconvulsive therapeutic sessions and travels to over a hundred cities all over the world in a completely manic phase, I have often asked:

What if the person Who You Are, the true you suffers from a mental illness?

Clinical depression, bipolar disorder, anxiety, nymphomania, anti-social personality disorder, schizophrenia, insomnia, multiple personality disorder, the list of mental illnesses could go on and on. Mental illness is prevalent, and the amount of suffering that it creates is greatly substantial. Just as addiction destroys lives, mental illness causes as much, if not sometimes more suffering in terms of intensity and prevalence.

So what of it? Why in the world would someone want to be Who They Are when Who They Are is, by societal standards, insane? Where can there be Self-acceptance, Self Love, and Self compassion?

Both unfortunately and fortunately, a part of the problem doesn't come from Who You Are, but instead, it comes from what everyone else assumes you to be. Those with mental illnesses can be especially hard on themselves as well, expressing guilt and shame, a desire to be a "normal" person with a healthy mind, heart, and soul. The hallucinations, feelings of grandeur, feelings of depression, and everything that comes with mental illness, can surely suck, destroy your life and your relationships, and elicit hardships that only you can understand in its entirety.

To once again bring back the same metaphor, only those who have experienced mental illness, just as those who have burnt their hand over the candle, can truly understand what it means to live with a mental illness. Otherwise, it is just words, descriptions, assumptions, and projections. You know Yourself better than anyone, and although I myself have been living with bipolar disorder for the greater part of my life, I can't pretend that I understand what you are going through, what you have been through, and what may come for you in the future.

Thus, while living in a culture that has a certain stigma regarding mental illness, which is not always informed or compassionate, your inner critic, your ego, is always fed with constant bouts of negativity.

Well, both Monk Xu and myself, along with thousands of others, are here to say otherwise, and we are not saying that your mental illness has a positive reason and that you should be happy with the cards you were given; instead, we are saying that we Love you just the Way You Are. No matter what, we have the highest thoughts about you, and by cultivating your mind, being aware of Yourself while having the highest thoughts of Yourself as well, you can also see the Love within you.

Recognising weakness and acceptance of it

When living with a mental illness, even though you have the highest thoughts of Yourself and accept the Love that is within you, your symptoms are going to flair up; mine do almost every day. You are going to feel depressed, your manic phases are going to manifest themselves, you may begin hearing things, you may want to go and have sex with everyone you meet, you may wake up in places and have no idea how you got there, and so on.

Thus, in regards to your condition and the effects that it has on your ability to Love yourself, you must Love yourself enough to get help, see a therapist, and perhaps, try different medications. But no matter what you do, never have any Fear. You are the Way You Are, and you can be nothing else.

Fear is not going to get you anywhere. It will not bring you a peaceful state of mind. Fear only makes you lose your way.

Objectively examine your situation, watch your thoughts and breathe. Be One with yourself and Reality, the *Now*, and if you discover that you don't like something about yourself, take every thought that you have of guilt, "why-me," shame, and tell yourself, "I am Who I Am, and Who I Am is on a never-ending journey of improvement and Self-acceptance."

Face your struggles with Love and courage, but remember, they are only struggles if you consider them to be a struggle. As a proposition, consider them to be an opportunity, an experience, to discover and be Who You Are.

And furthermore, remember the key word in mental illness: *illness*. It is a biomedical component. Nothing is your fault, and you absolutely deserve the compassion that you see within Yourself. You are not flawed, weak, or attract poor choices. On the other hand, you are given an opportunity, an experience, to utilise strength and empowerment in profound ways, and in the conflict of darkness in your life, the balance and equilibrium of the Universe makes it so that the Light in your life is just as profound; you just have to accept darkness, just as you accept the Light.

In courage and Love, and not in Fear, you must cultivate healthy habits, seek professional help if needed, and make sure that you realise that in order to engage the Love that already exists in the world, you must start from within.

And within, you need to remember the most important part of Yourself, just like how constantly thinking about a headache makes it that much more interfering and stressful, thinking that your Identity, Who You Are, and your mental illness in the same light only enhances the distress that much more.

I mean, who with a mental illness walks around with a badge on their shirt or a big sign over their head claiming to the world that they are mentally sick? As it is on the outside, there needs to be balance on the inside, and thus don't walk around with a sign on the inside of Yourself, a blow horn screaming out, that You are mental illness in sneakers. You are Who You Are, and You are not the labels, the assumptions, placed upon you.

However, just because you don't walk around without a sign stating your identity as mental illness on the outside or the inside, you cannot pretend that your mental illness doesn't exist.

You can't escape Reality, and although your mental illness isn't Who You Are, it is a part of your *Now*. When the time is right, when you feel that you need to talk to someone you trust, who doesn't cater to the misinformed stigmas regarding mental illness, explain this part of You with sincerity, and never, ever be ashamed of the universal wiring within your brain. Additionally, this also means that you cannot just imagine that you are a strong human, who through the power of the mind can overcome your mental afflictions.

Keep in mind that most, if not all, mental illness comes from a mineral and vitamin deficiency which may cause a mechanical dysfunction in the brain; it is through your mind and your thoughts, that this dysfunction presents itself. To understand this process requires great courage. Never underestimate the universal unfolding of how one may be unique in the making of being a miracle. Therefore, you also must accept the fact that you have weaknesses, especially in terms of your mental illness.

You are One with yourself, and in the Tao, there are no imperfections, there only *is*. A weakness, in the spirit of the duality of the Tao, is by **NO** means a bad thing. So many in the world preaches strength, dexterity, and casting away your sins so that you can be saved! However, where does strength and dexterity come from?

Within the relative, providing definition and meaning in everything in Reality, strength and dexterity come from weakness. Your weakness is not "bad," and nor is it "good." Examine your weakness, analyse your triggers, watch your mind and be still, and always express Love for yourself. Through weakness, you have a means of Self-improvement. If you ignore your weaknesses, you have nowhere to start.

Listen to your mind, dissolve the illusions and the stigma regarding your illness, and meditate (which is described later in this book). The journey within furthers Self-acceptance, and by first accepting Yourself, others can accept Who You Are, as well. By Loving Yourself, others can Love Who You Are as well.

But lastly, and most importantly, always have the highest thoughts of Yourself and always do what you think will be the best thing for you. Never Fear, listen and contemplate what others say, but never lose sight of Yourself when constantly improving from the throes of mental illness.

If you think therapy and medication is the best thing for you, then do it, embrace the experience, and continue listening to your mind, body, and soul. If your symptoms continue and you still cannot find Love or Self-acceptance for Yourself, try something else.

Like I said in the beginning, You can only be You, but you are not mental illness, and to be You, it all comes down to Love.

Chapter 8

Balance, Equilibrium, and Strength

Nothing in life stays fixed—everything moves and the nothingness in all things is 'still'. This stillness gives strength and balance to all to which we consider equilibrium.

—Monk Xu

Light and dark, Love and Fear, black and white, like and dislike, receive from above and give back to the Earth, chaos and order, ease and tension, concrete and imaginary, and so on; balance and equilibrium is and always will be the persistent conflict endearing in the Universe. Nothing within the finite world, that is apart from the Infinite, remains the same as is, and if we could say one Truth about life and Reality we would say that it changes.

Everything is in a Perpetual State of Creation

All of which you see around you, be it snow-capped mountains, a bowl of sugar-covered strawberries, your lover relaxing in a sun chair, or even a difficult breakup or heartbreak is not only a product of Creation, but these things are also Creators themselves. Whether your idea of Creation is that from God or through the process of millions of years of evolution and the transference of energy, every piece of Reality has a role in further Creation. The mountains on the hill, underneath an exploding red and orange sky, is a Creator, as you can say that it creates the image of Beauty in your heart, creates warm and fuzzy feelings. A breakup, the Creation of mismatched personalities and an imbalance in self-Love and Love for others, creates the feelings of sadness and emptiness, of which could only be possible if you have once felt great happiness and fulfilment in your life or relationship. The painting or the poem you create serves then to create a message or relaxation or simple enjoyment for those who see or read it. Your lover creates Love within you, your apples create pleasure on your taste buds, your electronics create enjoyment or productivity, your friends create companionship.

For many, the continual cyclic nature of a Creator that creates a Creation, which is also a Creator that creates as well, is the great equilibrium of life. It is the cycle of balance.

In the speed of life, with a hundred tasks covering the moment we wake until we try and close our eyes, it is surprising how often our plans for the day are balanced and pleasant, and yet so much is put off for later. You want to go for a run, enjoy your hobbies, relax and take a tea with sugar, call your Mum, stop an addiction, see your friends, be fit and so forth. I believe the intentions for balance are always there, but due to our obligations, our bills and caring for ourselves and dependents, the balance goes completely out the window. We no longer listen to what our mind, body, and soul are saying, and the equilibrium is shattered.

Imbalance Furthers our Attachments

With no balance, no equilibrium, we are continually trying to reach balance in the same mode of effortlessness that gravity holds us to the ground (I've never heard gravity complain about its monumental tasks), but with so many tasks and things to do, we rush through our obligations with great velocity, with no awareness, desperate for balance (I've heard many complain that there just isn't enough time in the day). The scales are tipped and many people often go into "program mode" to get through the day, or the desire to get things done without awareness and for the sole purpose of trying to maintain an equilibrium. When going throughout your day in a "program," doing what you have to do but not wanting to do it so you "buck up" and bite your tongue, looking out the window to watch the clouds go by with a mind a million kilometres away, you are no longer Creating either.

Your focus fades on the tasks at hand, the enjoyment falters, and the things you do have no purpose except to try and restore the balance. After a long day of work, washing the dishes slowly, with awareness, is difficult when all you want to do is relax (maintain the balance between work and relaxation). Of course, much of our work lives are used to make money or feed the families, we think we don't have a choice, and then when going through your days in a "program" to restore balance, you are in the process of sacrificing your Reality, the Who You Are, as opposed to being one with yourself and everything around you, diving into the Love of the world as opposed to withholding a Fear of "not-enough-time."

Such sacrifice that you make also creates expectations and results, and in this imbalance where sacrifice is needed, the results are things that we want to hold on to. We become attached to our own Creations as we gave up so much to create them. Many create their wealth while sacrificing time and health, and then lock all of their wealth away and let it create interest, which is then also locked away, and thus refusing the wealth's ability to be a Creator for others as well as yourself. We create Love with another person, and because of our imbalance of Love without this person, we hold dearly onto them, often squeezing so tight their heads pop right off.

Imbalance furthers our attachment, our Fear of separation and our distance from noticing the moment and being grateful for everything that exists in the *Now*.

The importance of maintaining balance on a daily basis cannot be understated, and it affects literally every part of your life. Moreover, it affects your ability to remain in the *Now* and be Who You Are, as well as make conscious decisions for every second of your day.

Balance, on the other hand, allows you to swim with the rivers of Life, and never against the *Flow*.

Thus, when seeking to balance your life, especially when you work 8 to 12 hours a day to barely make the rent or pay the pills or conduct the millions of tasks that parents must do, there are five crucial realms that you should always consider:

1. Sleep
2. Work
3. Eating
4. Emotional Expression of Self
5. Play

Also known throughout psychology circles as S.W.E.E.P. These five elements of life are the basic integral laws of balance in a modern day world, and over-indulging one creates rifts in the others and all benefits of balance are hampered.

Although each aspect of S.W.E.E.P. requires the same amount of focus and attention, the one element that receives the least attention is definitely sleep. Yes, I know we have millions of things to do, lives to live, and money and careers to tend to, but without quality sleep, your value of Creation is lazy and rushed. It's unfortunate, but sleep is often the only time of the day that people relax as well, and when it comes time to rest your head on the pillow, all of your thoughts and stressors from a busy day come rushing into your mind, interrupting your ability to feel the bedsheets over your body, hear the ambient sounds of the night (or day), and listen to the fatigue of your body, mind, and soul.

Secondly, as we all work to be successful, care for our dependents, create independence with the aid of monetary value, put food on the table and a roof over our heads, work is the second most imbalanced portion of many of our lives.

But, you ask, with normal workdays taking up eight hours in a 24-hour day, how is it possible to balance? Many of us work full-time, go to school, care for a family, and some even work a second job just to make ends meet. It may seem that in our society, maintaining a balance that the Universe requires cannot be done, but even with work, it is all about being aware of our Reality, investing our minds in Creation, and changing the way we think about being at work.

For example, if you dread being at work all day, feel a constant sleepiness and make the clock your God (which could also be an effect from imbalance caused by lack of sleep), and fake your smiles to each person you see, then yes, "work" is going to create imbalance.

If we were to take a look at the day of Monk Xu, who, in my opinion, is much more busy than many of us, we not only see several elements of Creation, but through his tenants of discipline and serenity, awareness in the *Now*, he is able to maintain complete balance, catering his mind and furthering his Creation within the world. Let's take a look at part of his schedule:

The Day in a life of a Monk—or—Anyone Who Becomes Harmonious

Before you even open your eyes, but feel that you are now awake, lie still, watch the activity of your mind. Is it suddenly filled with anxiety and Fear of not enough time? Do you hear the words, "You gotta, gotta, gotta?"

This is normal, and especially normal if there are many things to do throughout the day. Denying this normality is denying your Reality. So, just watch these thoughts. Notice their presence, but do not react to them.

Breathe. Quiet and still your mind.

Tell yourself that all of these things will be done. There is no need to worry. You have no idea how your day will resolve, and your assumptions are merely imaginations. Pay attention to the *Now*, pay attention to the activity of the mind. But do not react.

Then, first things first: your body is tired and tight after a full night's rest. Stretch.

Stretch your body, because you are surely going to need your body throughout the day, even if you are just sitting in a cubicle. Arms overhead and legs extended, and stretch. And breathe deeply. Feel the new air of the day reach your lungs, sending oxygen to each of your muscles to wake them and relax them at the same time.

Get off the bed, place your feet on the floor, and continue stretching your entire body. Stretch your feet, your neck, your arms and legs. Stretch your back and your hamstrings.

Every time that you get up. Vitalise every body part by breathing and go slow. The reservoir of where energy comes from is free and abundant.

If your girlfriend, boyfriend, spouse, or newfound lover who you are confused about, looks at you oddly with all of your stretching and breathing, don't give a damn, because through simple stretching, a still mind, right when you wake up, you are already on a path of being Who You Are throughout the day. And being You is the best (and only) thing that you can do. If you are feeling good about what you're doing, and you're doing it for your spirit, then just do it and don't second-guess yourself. Furthermore, if you have been sleeping well (the first element of balance), then you won't want to roll over under your covers and sleep until your second alarm goes off five minutes later.

Be a bell in your stance to life. Yet never wait for the second alarm bell to get you out of bed.

Typically, Monk Xu heads outside for some Qi Gong to release built up energy and anxiety, to get his body moving in gear, and to quiet my mind. I would recommend Qi Gong to anyone, but if you prefer to run, do an hour of Yoga, pull-ups or push-ups, or any sort of physical activity, then do that. Your body needs to move when you wake up to initiate the momentum of energy throughout the day.

As you have breakfast, eat very slowly. Be aware of every bite, and chew your food completely. There's a reason that food tastes good, it's pleasurable, and so dive into the pleasure, the almost sexual energy that food elicits as it squirms on our taste buds. Bite and feel every taste, every texture.

Always have some fruit as well.

Every couple of hours throughout your day, eat something (remember the Eat of S.W.E.E.P.), and eat in mindfulness, clearing your mind while giving your metabolism continual energy. Eating three large meals a day, the imbalance, strikes fear to your metabolism, as it's unsure of when you'll be eating again, and thus the food is stored and you feel sleepy and tired.

After breakfast, work for a full 2 ½ hours in complete mindfulness, paying attention to your tasks and being aware of your Creations. After 2 ½ hours, take fifteen minutes for a cup of tea, a glass of water, a quick walk around the office or a stare out the window, but make sure that your stare isn't empty—notice the clouds, the sky, everything around you. Then, work 2-½ hours again and take a break for lunch.

As you can see from just Monk Xu's morning, we have complete balance that all starts with the quality of sleep that you receive. Eating well and utilising work for emotional expression, putting in some time for play and exercise, all of this is not an easy thing to do, and it requires absolute discipline and awareness in every choice that you make.

To create discipline in your life, establishing awareness and conscious decision-making, to maintain balance and release your soul from the prisons of modern life, you can start with one activity:

Meditation and stillness is watching the breath. True meditation simply means to give 100% attention to anything at hand.

Chapter 9

Meditation and the Inward Journey

It is possible to experience anything with the mind. To experience the flight of a bird. To know what it is to be a rock, an animal or a tree. To feel the space within a room, in every person and all things within it, as one. To be the earth or the infinite universe. We have the potentiality of Gods and will not find true fulfilment with anything less.

—Monk Xu

Experience the mind by journeying within

Always having something in front of our faces, something going into our ears, something flashing across our eyes, is certainly not a new phenomenon in the digital age. Surely, like many I know, you may be sickened by the family dinner table whereas everyone under the age of 18 is clicking away on their smartphones or tablets, whereas the two lovers sitting next to one another talk through texts, whereas the downtown streets present hundreds talking on cell phones or plugging their ears with headphones. I may be putting this information in a "bad" light, and you may be able to see my frustration in the fact that stories of people getting hit by cars or walking off cliffs because they didn't take a moment to look up from a screen and notice the world around them.

Yes, it bothers me. But it shouldn't, because it is neither "bad" nor is it "good." If you look down upon those always on a smartphone, while you relax in front of the television drinking wine, or reading your favourite book all night long, or reading the newspaper while eating breakfast, then what, may I ask, is the difference? All of it, including smartphone or tablet addiction, is still a constant focus on our outside world, and a distancing from the inside of you.

When all is Oneness, the inside of you and the outside are the same, and so energy should be delivered to both to facilitate harmony. It is important to remember that the digital is neither "bad" nor "good," it just is and it is up to you whether you look upon it in Fear or in Love.

Like we mentioned in the last chapter, there needs to be balance, a combination of looking both outwards and within, being one with Reality while being one with yourself, listening to the world speak and breathe while listening to your mind, body, and spirit speak and breathe. To create the balance that gives and receives, that allows you to be Who You Are both inside and out, you need to still the mind, eliminate the outside, and listen to the inside.

In other words, you need to meditate and still the mind.

Crystalise the Now

Of course, you don't have to do anything, and if you have a better method of listening to yourself and quieting the mind, then by all means, actively listen to what your body, mind, and soul is telling you.

However, despite the common misconception about meditation, anything that you do that allows you to actively listen to what your body, mind, and soul is telling you *is* meditation.

Sitting in the lotus position, middle finger and the thumb in connection, and exhaling loud *ooooohhhhhmmmmmssss* may or may not be meditation. It all depends on what works for you. Therefore, if you want to crawl into the foetal position and if this is comfortable and allows you to meditate, then go ahead. Meditation is your personal journey within, to watch your thoughts, discover and be Who You Are, and completely eliminate the Fear from your disposition.

In a nutshell, to meditate there are three things that you need to do:

1. Get into a comfortable position
2. Remove yourself from anything that may distract you, such as the television, your cell phone, and people who may not respect the action you are taking to greatly improve your life. Also, you can turn all of this stuff on later, but for now, let's just focus on you.
3. Watch your breath go slowly in and out

You can close your eyes, or you can keep them open, but when open, make sure that all of your attention is focused upon your breath, and not what your eyes are seeing.

Feel the breath flowing in through your nostrils, filling and filling your lungs, take a slow, calm, and comfortable deep breath. Let your chest rise, your lungs are full with life-giving oxygen, your alveoli is absorbing the oxygen and your circulatory system is sending oxygen to every muscle, organ, and basically, part of your body.

Oxygen relaxes.

Your body relaxes.

You relax.

And the mind stills.

Keep the focus on your breath, breathe in and out again and again, over and over, feel the air filling your lungs and spreading throughout your body and exhale the excess out. This is not easy, and whether you have never done this before or you've meditated every day for five years, your thoughts are going to stray. As if automatically, you'll start thinking about how stupid you look, the things you have to do right after meditating, that time five years ago when you lost that argument but came up with the perfect comeback 10 minutes after the occurrence, and anything else that your brain will pump into your conscious mind.

This is normal, and when you notice that you haven't noticed your breathing for a while, don't be upset or frustrated. Remember that there is no "good" or "bad," no "right way" or "wrong way," there is simply acknowledgement. Be aware of the fact that you are not focusing on your breath, and return your awareness to your breathing. Five breaths later, you may once again lose focus and dive into your thoughts, and this is fine, this is normal. But simply return your focus to your breath once you notice that you've transferred your attention to your thoughts.

This is meditation, and there is nothing more to it.

But I'll mention again, it is not easy. It requires discipline, sincerity, and most importantly, it requires absolute faith that what you are doing, your quieting the mind, is helping you be Who You Are, to eliminate the Fear and replace it with Love, to expel stress and be in Oneness.

After meditating for a couple of months, you may notice some small changes, you may find yourself more focused, more disciplined, more aware of what you are thinking and Who You Are, but these changes might be small, and therefore, there can be no expectations.

If you go into your meditation thinking it will improve your sociability, it won't. If you go into meditation thinking it will bring you closer to Who You Are, it won't. There can be no expectations or assumptions about what meditation will bring you, and in its fundamental purpose, it is a moment for you to slow down, relax, focus on your breath, and be calm and still. Simply put, enjoy the journey, and drop everything—assumptions and expectations by simply letting it all go.

But once again, when you are first starting to meditate, it can be stressful. So many things to do in the day and no time to do them, and here you are, doing "nothing" with your eyes closed (or open), watching your breath. After two minutes, after losing focus on your breath and your awareness turns to your thoughts of what you need, what you desire, what you must do, it is easy to start feeling the stress rise within you, hardening your blood, and after a minute of doing "nothing," of meditating, you stop and go about your day.

Of course one minute of meditating is much better than no minutes of meditation, but remember, maintain the balance. In terms of pure meditation, without outside distractions, it can help to start with five minutes in the morning and once again before going to bed. If you ever start feeling stressed that you have so many things to do in the day, just keep in mind that 10 minutes out of 1,440 minutes in a day is really nothing.

That would be like having $1,440 in your pocket but refusing to spend $10 on a nice meal. Don't be cheap with your time, and no matter what you do in your life, you are never, never, never wasting time.

"The Now" cannot ever be wasted as "It" will always be there to save you from illusion, if you let it.

—Monk Xu

Honestly, time doesn't care what you do. Time cannot be wasted. And most importantly, you cannot "save" time.

So, spend 10 minutes of your day at first, and after you start feeling comfortable, after you discover that you can spend 5 minutes of sitting without losing concentration on your breath, then increase the time a little more, and a little more. Maintain the balance, keep the harmony, and always do it with Love.

Also, if your meditation still feels rushed, set a timer for five minutes, and trust that the timer will tell you when you should then go about your day.

There is, however, one condition where you should stop meditating. When the moment that you feel tired, that being comfortable and watching your breath, is making you fall asleep, then stop meditating, because you are no longer meditating.

I'll never forget what a teacher once told me: whenever you are meditating, you should maintain the same amount of alertness that would you give when driving a car on slippery roads in the middle of a blizzard.

If you are falling asleep while meditating, then your equilibrium is already off. Get some sleep.

This inward journey, through meditation, also transfers into every part of your life, and most importantly, it allows you to experience the world as it is, without conscious and subconscious judgements, and without Fear. You can watch your breath everywhere, at any moment of the day; as compared to food or water, you won't survive very long without oxygen. It is the force, the energy, and the equilibrium of Nature that brings life and Love. Breathing is Reality, as whether you know it or not, you are always breathing.

Only when one gives indication to the depth of breath— only then does one know that they are breathing at all.

Thus, you can meditate when you go for a walk, just watch your breath. You can meditate when you speak with friends, just watch your breath. You can meditate when you, well, do anything at all, just watch your breath. And furthermore, watching your breath as you conduct other things doesn't take you away from outside occurrences. While speaking with a friend and watching your breath, you can still hear and consider what your friend is saying, but while watching your breath, you quiet the thoughts, assumptions, and imaginations that you may have, and *Bam!,* you are right in the moment. You are One with your friend, your answers are considered and not obstructed by rambling thought, both his or her words and your words are clear.

The window is clean, and you become one with Reality, with the *Now,* and thus, you *Flow.*

Through meditation, you eliminate the Fear that you have throughout life. No longer will you be afraid of all the things you have to do, afraid of the "limited" time that you think you have, afraid of sickness and old age, afraid of looking stupid and being uncool, afraid of loss and separation, afraid of losing all of your possessions and wealth, and everything in between.

Eliminate the stress and the Fear, and your body, mind, and soul rejoices in equilibrium, and the most prominent, profound, and beautiful result? Your Creative energy maximises, and regardless of what you do, you do it with joy, innovation, and simple happiness.

And most of all, you do it all effortlessly.

When you're peaceful, you wash the dishes well, you love your spouse well, you see the beauty of a sunset in everything that you do.

Meditation is a continual inward journey, a process, and it neither takes you away from the world nor locks you in the throes of your mind. Instead, it makes you Who You Are, and you react to the world around you just as the world reacts to gravity.

Sit or stand, lie down or go for a walk, do whatever you like that makes you feel comfortable, but never forget to be watchful with your breath.

And unless you are dead, your brain won't forget to breathe; you'll always be breathing, and so you might as well pay attention to it, become one with your mind, spirit, and body, and explode with harmony and equilibrium, and thus, you are in the *Now*.

Chapter 10

Finding Peace

Peace flowers fully when stillness is its catalyst.

—**Monk Xu**

Unifying order and chaos through peace

When asked about the current state of the world, the Reality in which we live in, rarely does one immediately jump to:

"Oh, it's such a peaceful world!"

"There is joy around every corner, and when we open up our hearts, we ride rainbows into our imagination and graze with unicorns."

Wars seem to be in continuation, our notion of evil always triumphs, little children are being executed at gunpoint in American schools, the blood of hundreds of thousands soaks the sand and soil in Syria, our lives are muddied with the struggle for work and sustenance, celebration and social acceptance in exchange for casting away our intuition, homelessness and severe drug abuse runs rampant, we are lonely, afraid of death, cancer and AIDS. At first look, the world doesn't seem like a very peaceful place, and it is quite easy to jump on the bandwagon of The End of Times is here! Our sins and debauchery must have repercussions, and either God or Nature is really pissed off.

Be honest, how many of you have wished for a global zombie epidemic just because it would eliminate the boredom of our society, give you the chance to run wild with a chainsaw and cutting off heads?

When your focus, your Reality and your *Now*, is bent on the destruction and idiocy of the human race, is always tuning in to the death and tragedy, what does that say about Who You Are? Everything that you do, that you inherit from within and without, comes from a thousand little decisions that you make throughout your day, and by choosing to concentrate on hate and evil, you do not acknowledge the world as it is, you judge the world based on assumptions and projections that you have, and you imagine the world as you would like to see it.

But you can't pretend that "evil" doesn't exist, as by pretending that evil doesn't exist, you are then presenting that Love doesn't exist either, for everything in the Universe is based off balance. By not understanding Love, how can you look at something and call it evil? By not understanding evil, how can you look at something and call it Love?

Furthermore, you cannot look at the occurrences of the world and stand by idly, as often you have no choice about how to feel about certain events, and therefore, by looking at something that you believe is evil and calling it, with words and action, "evil," you are then discovering what about You is Love. In other words, your classifications of evil determine Who You Are and who you want to be in this Universe.

In respect to balance, be aware of all of the evil in world, looking upon it in understanding, confidence, and stillness instead of Fear, and also spend just as much time being aware of the peace in the world.

The media loves to interpret and dissect the story of the Boston Bombers or the war in Syria, but at the same time, it never dissects the story of the boy sitting on top of a hill, under the sunlight, with his arm around his dog, Twinkles. Why isn't there a weekly segment called Teenagers in Love? Why does a program that involves a bunch of people yelling at each other typically garner higher ratings than a group of people having lunch under the palm trees?

Why?

Because we like conflict; it's exciting and scary and gets a whole range of chemicals and emotions rampaging through our bodies.

Be Less Enamoured by Conflict

Conflict is the duality, the Ying and Yang, the black and white, rubbing up against one another to give us meaning and definition. If you look up into the sky, the Universe is certainly not a peaceful place at times, with supernovas scorching entire solar systems, black holes with unparalleled force of gravity eating away at the substance of our stars, our moon created from a violent impact on the Earth, and so on. This violence, this lack of peace, is also the cause for Creation, and so as it is in the Universe, it is also on Earth.

Through war we sometimes topple evil and bring peace, through the experience of hate we can cater a better understanding of Love, through the Fear of night we produce a joy of the day, through work we adore relaxation, through loneliness we learn to Love ourselves so that others may Love us too, and so forth.

Few people look at war and see peace within the fighting and bloodshed, as sometimes our faith is shattered in view of such atrocity, and Fear overwhelms. Few people look at a couple fighting, yelling at one another over dinner, and see peace, as we forget that each soul is in the process of learning about Who It Is.

Through meditation and the cultivation of the Mind, of the inner You, and of the *Now*, you can change the way that you look at things. You can see violence and evil, but you can choose to also see the duality within the action, the "good" and the "bad" in both sides, the soul and collective consciousness in discovery. Or, if you so choose, you can see Fear, live in Fear, and be just that: Fear.

Fear does not still the mind, it pokes at the fires of assumption and projection, it showcases an imbalance of your view of the Universe, and it locks you away, separates you, and makes you attached to what you own and what you have.

But how, how, how, how, was the Holocaust and WWII a "good" thing? What could possibly be good about the extermination of millions, the creation of the Cold War and the race for nuclear arms, the exodus of Jewish peoples to Palestine and Israel, and the half-century and onwards conflict that has been nothing but a stalemate of bloodshed and hate? How is it possibly to look at something like this and feel peace?

Practice Self-Acceptance and Love

It may be hard to believe, but peace only comes from within. Nothing, absolutely nothing, in the outside world is a Creator of peace. You, and only you, create the peace that you see in the world. Peace comes from Love, and if you can't find Love in yourself, you won't find peace anywhere.

In a situation such as the Holocaust or WWII, the cold war and nuclear arms race, the Israeli-Palestinian conflict, and anything else in this world that we consider as "evil," it is important to never turn away from these matters. You cannot look away from Reality, because Reality is all there ever was, is, and will be. By looking away, focusing your attention on other things because you don't want to accept what is happening in the world, you are also turning away from the conflict in the Universe. If you turn away from conflict, you then turn away from peace as well. You can't turn away from what scares you, but you can choose to be Love as opposed to Fear.

Stated in other words, you bring the peace into this world that you see. Although it's hard to believe because you are just a single person in the world of 7+ billion, that your view of peace within yourself so that you can discover peace elsewhere doesn't matter in the grand picture of things, by being Who You Are you inspire others to do the same. Conflict in the Universe is natural, our solar system was born out of incredible violence, but whether you choose peace within yourself or Fear, it is entirely up to you.

From the harmony of thought, word, and deed, your every activity, every decision that you make, determines the degree of peace that you create, and your Creation of peace serves to be a Creator of further peace, and so on the cycle goes. With bloodshed and hate all around you, while maintaining a still mind that ensures confidence instead of Fear, the way in which you express Who You Are can create peace for others. When you see peace in yourself, you see the band Tanjaret Daghet from Syria, a group of three musicians performing music at the Lebanon's Child Friendly Spaces of a UNHCR refugee-registration zone, allowing children to clap, sing, and dance together. You see a photo of a Filipino boy struggling through water and floods that have risen above his knees, in the midst of the devastating Typhoon Haiyan, carrying his dog on his back. You see stories like that of Daniel Black, who broke his neck in 2009 and set about raising £22,000 for a surgery that would allow him to walk again. When hearing of a story about a six-year-old boy with cerebral palsy, who also needed a surgery, Daniel gave the young boy every penny that he had raised, saying, "For me, things are not getting better soon. I wanted to help someone whose life could get better."

If Daniel, if Tanjaret Daghet, if the boy with the dog on his back, had only saw Fear in the conflicts at hand, and could see no peace within themselves, had not put their thought, word, and deed in equilibrium, were not still or confident in their minds, then they might not have produced the peace in the world that they saw within themselves.

These three stories are certainly just a drop in the bucket of worldwide kindness and selfless acts of joy, but solely from these three, we can discover a common factor: Self-acceptance.

By accepting the Self, you accept the events and occurrences in the world for as they are, and by letting go of the judgements and the Fear, the Self *acts*, in the *Now*, along with the *Flow*, and creates peace in the outside just as it is peace on the inside.

The journey to Self-acceptance, by being Who You Are in thought, word, and deed, is only as long as you allow it to be. Let go of the past, remember that the future doesn't exist, and be a Self-centred individual.

Not an egotist, but always put yourself first and foremost. Within Love and relationships, hardships, struggles, and difficulties, it is only the Love and peace that you see and feel within yourself that transmits to the outer the world, as both are one in the same.

You are not separated from this world, you are not a vessel on a road trip, carrying your mind in the cockpit. You are the Universe. Whether created from your God or from the incredible struggle and violence that occurred when your father shot millions of sperm, all of whom were fighting, to reach your mother's egg, and the evolution from a single cell to trillions, you are a Miracle. Thus, what is inner is outer. Your inner view is your outer view. You actively focus on being Who You Are, to be a better person unobstructed by Fear, you then see that others are doing the same, whether consciously or subconsciously.

We are all trying to evolve. Every soul of a human, just like the soul of every animal, or every tree, evolves.

Trees bend and twist so that their leaves receive the most sunlight; if a tree Feared that there would not be enough sunlight in the middle of the forest, then it would not do everything that it could to touch the rays of the sun, to touch the rays of Life.

Self-acceptance, and peace, and Love, and being Who You Are who lives in the *Now*, is always the tree evolving to reach the sunlight. It's not easy, and you might have to twist and bend to get there, but always remember that, like the tree, the process is effortless as long as you are being You.

Still the mind, discover the inner peace and the Love that you have for yourself, and within the conflicts of the Universe, the conflicts of this world, the natural conflicts of Reality, You are a beacon of peace and Love in thought, word, and deed.

And so peace reigned this chapter. Let's end with a famous quote from Jimi Hendrix:

"When the power love overcomes the love of power, the world will know peace."

Chapter 11

Harnessing the Collective Good

A human being is a part of the whole called by us as the universe. We are a part limited in time and space. He experiences himself, his thoughts and feeling as something separated from the rest, a kind of optical delusion of his consciousness. This delusion is a kind of prison for us, restricting us to our personal desires and to affection for a few persons nearest to us. Our task must be to free ourselves from this prison by widening our circle of compassion to embrace all living creatures and the whole of nature in its beauty.

—Albert Einstein

Defining compassion to be able to live it

There are times when I am walking, thinking about my day, my past or future, about my friends and family, and just thinking, but when I look down and see my legs, feel how my arms are moving when I walk, it all looks and feels so very strange when I give these things my attention. Naturally, without any focus, my arms and legs just move as they always have been and always will, but as I try to describe the movements in my mind, my arms tighten up, I start swinging them wildly or hold them tight to my side, and all of a sudden I no longer know if I am walking or running. In the essence of walking, it is certainly better to just let in be, realise that I am walking and not think too much of it, or else things become so darn unnatural.

Just go with the *Flow*, and walk.

However, the more that I think about Love, the more that I try and describe Love and examine how it moves, analysing and hypothesising and making assumptions, the more Love feels like a program, something that is the result of a cause and effect.

If I do this, I believe I cause Love. Just like baking causes cupcakes, or work causes money.

The more I try to describe and analyse Love, the more I realise that it is one of those things that when you experience it, you most definitely know it, just like walking, just like anything that is Natural.

Thus, whenever either myself or Monk Xu are asked, "How can I become more compassionate in my life?" Or, "What is compassion?" The answer is often tricky, and it resembles describing Love.

According to the Merriam-Webster dictionary, the basic definition of compassion goes as follows:

A feeling of wanting to help someone who is sick, hungry, in trouble, etc.

Another definition from the same dictionary states:

Sympathetic consciousness of others' distress together with a desire to alleviate it.

The dictionary also states that *compassion* is also a noun, and I'm not sure what to do with both of these pieces of information.

Words describe, we hear and see things from others, we are told what things are and the role that they play in the universe, but how well does a love poem describe Love to someone who has never experienced Love before. The definition of compassion is fairly clear, and you can see how *compassion*, as a word, features both the will of solving a problem and being empathetic. Thus, it takes much more than being empathetic towards others' problems, and it involves a detection of this suffering and then action to solve it.

We see suffering all around us, and whether it is in the distress of someone's face, a mental, physical, or emotional anguish, through body language or someone telling you right to your face that he or she is suffering, the most simple and effortless part of compassion comes from the awareness that distress, tension, and pain of some sorts is involved.

But like Love, like compassion, like sticking your hand over the candle to discover the experience of being burnt, to truly understand the suffering of someone else, you must understand the suffering within yourself.

However, I don't mean that specifically. If someone is in emotional and physical pain because he or she has lost an arm, you don't need to go and cut off your own arm to feel what the other is feeling. Don't break up with your boyfriend or girlfriend just so that you can be compassionate towards your newly single friend. Instead, dive into your suffering and be aware of pain. How does the pain (physical, mental, or emotional) feel? What other areas of your life does this pain transmit towards? What does the pain, in the duality sense of the word, mean to you? Be aware of your pain, feel your pain, but remember to always do it with Love as opposed to Fear. Ensure the same modes of being Who You Are in regards of your own pain and be confident; do not judge, and just feel.

All are Born with the Desire to Evolve

Remember that everyone, every single soul that you come across, has been through some sort of suffering in his or her life. Every soul is trying to evolve, just as every tree bends and twists its branches in order to receive the sunlight. Look at the faces you see on the streets, and look beyond their images. Look beyond your idea of beauty or ugliness, beyond materialistic ideas of style or the way that people carry themselves, beyond religious affiliation, beyond sexual preference, beyond every detail on the surface. Do not look for the suffering in others, as all you will see is suffering, and when all you see is suffering, you do not see Love.

Look for the Love in every person you see, and no doubt, you will discover heartbreak, victory, success and failure, Love and hatred, Fear and confidence, joy, sadness, family, friendship, loneliness, interests, hobbies, passion, and every bit of the complexity that forms the consistency of Who You Are as well as Who We Are. We are all in this world together. We are all born from the same soil, the same desire to evolve. When you see the Love within yourself, you see the Love within others.

And then, as if something were in front of you this entire time but you didn't notice it, as it *was* in front of you this entire time, you see that Life, relationships, goals and dreams, the bulk of the things we do, is all for opportunity and experience. You see that no matter what, we try and put Ourselves into Reality, although our mind and our assumptions seem to tell us otherwise. And lastly, you feel compassion for every soul, every heart, and every mind that you see. No longer is there separation, as compassion is Universal and not exclusive. Groups, clicks, and labels no longer make any sense, as we are all, on the inside, trying to be the best people that we can be, and being the best that you can be is nothing more than being Who You Are.

Compassion is the highest thoughts that you can have about others, which always means having the highest thoughts for yourself, and when you can be One with both yourself and others, where all is evolution, you not only experience the empathy, see the struggle for Love in all, but also the solutions become clear. Perhaps with maybe a tweak here or there, depending on the specifics of the distress, you'll know the answer, because you have experienced it yourself.

Similar to meditation, similar to being Who You Are, similar to everything that we've discussed in this book, you can have no expectations or assumptions about what being compassionate will bring you. There is no end goal, there is no prize, no bag of candy sweets waiting for you afterwards, there is only the *Now*, and the collective good that compassion creates. For once you show compassion to others, they are able to actively experience what compassion is, without words and without definitions or assumptions of compassion.

From true compassion within yourself and then shown to others, you are, in a sense, holding someone's hand over the candle so that they can experience what it is like to be burnt. Once they have felt compassion, have experienced it themselves, then they are able to show compassion in others with much more sincerity and Love.

Unfortunately, this is not an automatic response, and not everyone even realises that they have experienced true compassion. However, showing compassion is like planting a seed of Love in others, and planting the seed is the only thing that you have control over. Whether the soil is good, it rains just enough, and the plant grows healthy is truly beyond your complete control.

Be Who You Really Are and Love Every Single Moment

You may not instigate change, and you should not actively seek to bring change. Be sincere about your compassion and your desire to be Who You Are in every situation, to be the Love that you feel within yourself. Being compassionate to "look" compassionate, and sexy, is basically a measure of your insecurity about Who You Are. You do not need applause and you do not even need to be noticed for what you do, but if it is given, always receive it with gratitude. There is nothing wrong with saying "You're welcome."

But no matter what you do, the compassion for others that you show, and the contribution to the collective good that you provide, never, ever, forget about the compassion that you must show yourself. This is an ongoing process, and you will be stuck with your own improvement, your being in the *Now* and the Who You Are, for the rest of your life.

Every day, every minute, and every decision in Monk Xu's life, as well as my life, is never seen as a challenge to be compassionate, to be sincere or disciplined, to be in the *Now*, but instead, it is seen as this great opportunity, perhaps the very opportunity of Life, to be Who We Are. Everything that you or I do is an expression, a Creation that comes from our heart, and it is a never ending opportunity to improve our thinking, our words, and our actions so that the "ego" is not touched by the negativity, the Fear, in the world. Instead, the negativity in the world, and our awareness of it, drives, pushes, screams in your face, for you to improve the collective good of us all.

So, the question remains as you come to finish line of this book, after all of this information and spiritual insight given by the venerable Monk Xu, what are you to do now?

Well, in a sentence, *Be Who You Are.*

Do not give up all of your things, all of your material possessions, quit your job, or doing anything extreme to find yourself. Those who live off bread and water, with no Earthly possessions, and who simply meditate all day long, may discover Who They Are and constantly live in the *Now*, but these types of people lack the opportunity and experience where you are able to define Yourself in all ways possible. Have children if you please, seek relationships and put all of your Love and awareness into that relationship. Do not be empty and seek fulfilment from people or things. Keep your mind still and empty and be complete. Seek success and utilise work to emotionally express Yourself. Do what you Love, your passion, and sure enough, you will become a master of it. Then, if you have mastered your passion because you enjoy doing it every day, someone will surely pay you for it.

You don't need to go and buy a plane ticket to visit monasteries or churches on the other side of the globe. The distance you travel on the outside has nothing to do with the distance you travel on the inside.

All of us have this hole in our stomachs, and so many try to fill it with money, relationships, religion, or possessions.

Seek challenges, opportunities, and experiences. Better Yourself. Always hold the highest thought of yourself, as the highest thought is Who You Are. Always hold the highest thoughts of others, and be compassionate, sincere, and disciplined in what you think, say, and do. Remember the collective good.

And *LIVE*.

LIVE until your heart can take no more, but always remain peaceful. Die peacefully with nothing left to say or do.

And *LOVE* each and every moment of your life, as the Reality is now, whether "good" or "bad." *LOVE* Yourself and everyone else, as you are all on this giant blue rock travelling hundreds of thousands of kilometres through the Universe, circling around a giant, fiery ball of light.

Look around.

LIVE.

And *LOVE*.

LIVE and *LOVE* with all of your heart, as if you really think about it, there's nothing else to do.

This is All that You are here for.

This is WHO YOU ARE and this is ALL THAT THERE IS.

THE END

Epilogue

Don't you just love happy endings? This is definitely one of those. Most especially because both our lives were not always peaceful and sublime. And we certainly were never this content before.

I have led a very turbulent life prior to meeting Monk Xu. In fact, I was tragically institutionalised ten times in psychiatric wards, most of the time in the solitary areas. I was abandoned by family and had to raise myself from 13 years old. At 16, I was forced to sell my body and soul to piranhas and vultures that were all too happy to take everything I had.

My life is now simple, I practice what we have written in this book.

We watch fervently and are careful to not fall into the traps of illusion. We love, we support and we cultivate daily.

Anyone that comes to the X A Q SHIN Sanctuary seeking spiritual awakening and wanting enlightenment are given the tools to find the Divine within. Over and over again, we open our hearts to those that want to connect. We watch ourselves flower in our service to the people. We smile from within as peace fills our life and contentment seeps through every part of our being.

Thank you for sharing this book with us and I sincerely hope you found exactly what you were looking for.

—Maria Pau and Monk Xu

This book serves as a manual to assassinate the ego. As stated in this book "The Now Is All There Is." and to this I'd like to add, "The Only Permanence in Life Is Change."

The essence of oneness is Universal and this unfolding expression of the road less travelled is truly the design of accepting and appreciating all that there is.

Once upon a time high up in the mountain I remember hearing from a gentleman who was knowledgeable and wise. He said: "The generations that follow is best taught by the living example."

Maria is definitely by far a leading example when it comes to not only changing people's lives by showing everyone on the path of change that there are endless possibilities to seeing and experiencing the beauty within. All the trials and tribulations on her triumphant journey have opened her heart to realms where miracles occur daily.

"The heart that forgives is the MIND and BODY that receives life's delicate gift; THE PRESENT; THE NOW."

I, Monk Xu, invite you right now to enjoy the most unforgettable treasure that is the blueprint within. What is the one thing on earth that every human being desires? It is a Universal desire throughout human history. It is so strong of a desire that humans have died for it and it is the greatest cause to fight for; yet it is the one idea that could unite all of humanity under the common cause. The best thing about this desire is the more we lose it the stronger the desire becomes. So what is this common desire?

IT IS FREEDOM.

Freedom may take many different personal paths but in the end we all want to control our own destiny—to live our own lives—to do what we want to do—to love who we want to love without others interfering. The SOUL is founded on this principal and it is the last beacon of hope throughout the world. Before the inward revolution—FEAR will always try to elude LOVE off its natural and just cause. This fear is promoted through our upbringing and is incessantly commercialised through media. The untouchable truth is right underneath your nose yet the first minute you are born—you are stamped and registered into slavery through what we call today; our birth certificate. If the torch of freedom is not realised then we numb ourselves by leading a robotic lifestyle that has no passion in it.

Here this book will liberate you and what I reiterate is— DO NOT BELIEVE THIS BOOK—Make up your own mind. Belief implies that there is a conclusion and in the true meaning of conclusion, the definition is that you have come to an END. Simply UNDERSTAND the book and take it upon yourself to LIVE and BE the TRUTH.

Please understand that I say through a fearless love—all things are effortless and that all things are possible. To rise to the highest potential is to see that by being CREATIVE— this evolution alone will unify your breath with all that there is. Happiness and contentment depend on your freedom. I am always available to ground your truth. Choose to be courageous and inevitably this virtue alone will keep you in peace and harmony.

As you finish this book, I am continuously creating and naturally expressing myself in all the ways I know and love. Training in the sanctuary of X A Q SHIN. Gardening is also one of my many passions. I find and make the time helping others and when I am troubled in thought (this also happens to me; I am HUMAN), I go on a random journey into NATURE and see the beauty in everything.

Take the time out one of these days and visit my website (www.monkxu.com) and feel free to peruse the pages. There you will find many pearls of truth that will liberate any Soul. Thank you for sharing our journey and I wish you many blessings.

—Monk Xu

Connect with Monk Xu at:

www.MonkXu.com

Support Maria's Award Winning Charity at:

wwwf.CoachingWithSubstance.org.au